Angels Watching Over Me

A New Age Odyssey

Kiros

A story told by the Author, Kiros, and written by Donna Martini

Edited by Donna Martini
Cover design by Aristea and Cheryl Edwards
Cover Photography by Aristea
Chakra illustration designed by Aristea and Kiros

Content Editors:

Craig Colasanti
Lisa Mongelli
Gina Califano

ISBN: 1508820287
ISBN 13: 9781508820284

Dedication

Special dedication to my parents who were my first teachers...
And to my children who will probably be my last...

To all the wonderful people in my life that have supported me with unconditional love, trust and faith, enabling me to courageously discover all that matters in life is to be who you truly are.

A most special dedication to the person who has inspired me to write this book and who's unique talents helped create the cover...Aristea, you are a beautiful soul, friend, and guide. I have endless appreciation, gratitude, and love, and I will honor and treasure our friendship forever.

Deep gratitude to all of the many teachers that I encountered who consciously or unconsciously helped me gain the wisdom to be able to 'teach unto others.'

Most importantly to God, all my ethereal Guides, the ArchAngels, Ascended Masters and Divine Beings, family, and friends...a huge thank you.

Lastly, to Donna Martini, whom without her help, skills and guidance, this book would not have come to fruition. I thank you for being you!

Note from the Writer

We sometimes meet people who touch us...teachers who bring such profound 'ah-ha' moments that along with those moments, the teacher remains with us forever. Kiros is one of those teachers. Since meeting him I have undergone my most amazing advancements in emotional and spiritual healing, and trust me, I am no stranger to healing methods! Ethereal energy, albeit intangible, represents the most stubborn ties and bonds we have between ourselves and those around us. Without his help I am not sure I could ever unravel the complexities of these connections or my life course. An additional bonus was being introduced to the ArchAngels and all the other ethereal Guides that are working on our behalf. I am convinced, they were an intrinsic part of my decision to help him bring this story to print. The main reason though was my desire to help others understand the disconnect we sometimes feel between our human and soulful selves.

As a wellness coach, I found clients, as well as myself, stuck in the same energetic patterns that seemed almost impossible to overcome. I consistently taught a method I call Positive Manipulation®, which is the spiritual process of converting any negative energy we physically, emotionally and mentally find ourselves in or around into a more positive and loving state of being. It was a proven method that helped so many people in so many ways, but there was a missing piece. Although I believed in the existence of what I thought of as "cords," I had no idea the degree in which we could become attached and more importantly, what those cords contained karmically. After Kiros told me of his work, I underwent the process myself and then sent client after client to experience the release. We all took great strides on our healing journey under his guidance, and I knew the rest of the world needed to know of his methods. It eventually became clear that we were led to one another for a higher purpose...a writer who desired to help others heal and a healer who desired to tell of his epic journey. A match that, apparently, heaven fully supported.

When the manuscript came to me in raw form, I was quite over-whelmed. Struggling with dyslexia since I was a young child, all I saw on each page were word after word of concepts and thoughts. They were like pearls of wisdom that needed to be strung together and made into something beautiful. I had been downloading information for years and translating what I heard into cohesive language, but I never tried to convey another person's thoughts and downloads. My worry was, "If I pull it apart to understand it, can I put it back together in his voice and leave his profound concepts in tact?" My love for Kiros and his teachings gave me the desire to at least try, and as I took on the challenge one sentence at a time, it became apparent that I didn't need more than will. A more profound and ethereal energy was helping me do the work. After a few days, I suddenly realized I was not challenged at all. I was energized! It was as if I was being lifted by the same angelic power that had been as-sisting him.

The Angels came through so much so, there were days that I couldn't stop writing! At six in the morning the alarm would go off, the coffee brewer was turned on and the writing would begin. Some days I would go on and on for sixteen hours with barely a break. I was filled with spir-it...his spirit...their spirit...my own spirit! I felt supercharged and blessed at the same time. The work flowed, and as Kiros and I collaborated on the final editing, a new synergy was established. He had years of teach-ing, heard brilliant messages and conceived beautiful concepts. I had the means to express them. Together we were able to convey what could transcend the confusion of the human self and bring out the soul voice in all of us. What started out as a gift I wanted to give to him, became the gift the Angels gave to me. I am so privileged to help bring this book to fruition. So excited to share the love and the beauty of this man's journey. So happy to spread the goodness with all of you.

Love and Healing Always, D
(Donna Martini)

Table of Contents

Part I

Part II

Part III

Introduction

When defining our life purpose, we need to look beyond the ordinary and the obvious...to those parts of our lives that didn't make sense, until one day, everything made sense. As I think back to my earliest memories, life started out as anything but ordinary. I was privileged to be raised in Athens, the birthplace of heroes and philosophers and a few miles from the Acropolis. My family expanded four generations of Athenians, and both my parents' childhood homes were only a few meters away from the Acropolis walls and the Agora. A beautiful and mystical place encircled by a distant chain of bare, rocky mountains and light blue sky, it echoed the wisdom of Socrates, Plato, Aristotle, Theseus, Pericles, just to name a few. Their wisdom and enlightened words continue to assist in the course of every philosopher's soul grooming, including my own. The pulse and radiance of nature on that part of our planet Earth is palpable and absorbed as a true life source. It inspires the mind as it magnifies the senses; it activates and transforms the heart as it awakens the spirit. Although it over flows with ancestry and can visually inspire through its time-worn landscape, no other place can make me feel so happy to be in the 'now,' than Greece. I have been truly blessed to have started life in such a magical place.

The two statements, "There are no mistakes" and "There's a reason for everything," are what inspired my inner quest for truth and knowledge about my real identity. Not just who or what I was, but also where I fit in humanity. Growing up, I was constantly aware of the energetic nuances in relationships with friends, siblings, and my many teachers...those that throughout the years have given me a lift up or a push down. I have questioned all of the good and not-so-good episodes I have encountered...those profound enough to have shaped my persona and create my human experience and those subtle enough to deserve a second look. All this led to the discovery of my life purpose.

I have always chosen to look at all events as pivotal points that redirect a journey. (Think of a map being stored in the subconscious mind detailing our most direct path.) Since all of us are partially in awareness throughout our lives at any given time, we choose what suits us best under each specific circumstance. Whether we are intentionally on a road of discovery or not, I truly believe wherever we are heading is absolutely the right place to travel. We will either learn the hard way or the easy way, but we will always be learning, and that is truth, my truth, and what inspired me to write this book. I hope it serves to help others discover easier ways to learn and grow on their own life odyssey.

The names used in my stories have been changed.

Part
I

Inspired by the Angels

Remembering my earliest childhood experiences, I realize now that most hours in my day were filled with the presence of Angels. And what extraordinary times they were! I immediately accepted the affection of the Angels and felt nourished and pampered by their presence. Our bond was effortless and in sync with the environment, creating a place of comfort, trust and belonging. My perception of their presence was what I would call the 'founding spark of how love ought to be.' It was an early introduction to self expression and awareness of love and most likely the reason for my desire to continually search for the same heavenly connection.

Angels are always around everyone, especially children, and some of us are lucky enough to keep the memories. My Angel interactions happened gradually, and I was always very comfortable around them, almost nonchalant. The first impression I have of interacting with the Angels was in persistent dreams about flying. These dreams would start with me trying to rise up off the floor, but in the dream my body wouldn't lift through the thick air, so I would pull all my core strength and leg energy to push off. Eventually, the flying became effortless as I was led to different locations. Instead of struggling, I was drawn into an area as if there was a vacuum pulling me where I needed to be.

Before long, I was flying all over the house, up and down in each room, over furniture, hovering by the ceiling, cruising over the dining table and kitchen counter. When I neared the front door though, I would catch a glimpse of sparkling eyes looking at me. Pretending that I didn't see them, I would continue on my flight. These friendly, shining eyes would follow me around persistently. They weren't scary to me though. They looked like happy, laughing eyes with a radiant glow that were backlit with colorful flashing lights.

The flying routine became predictable and always welcome. When they felt I was willing and ready, they allowed me to see a friendly face. Eventually, one of these glowing, floating like bodies with shimmering eyes became my friend—a friendship that endured my entire childhood. In play or alone with just my thoughts, the Angels were always there to keep me company. I could hear them speaking encouraging words to me, so I would answer them back. I was only about five, but had a great imagination and was putting it to good use by creating and building forts, airports, and houses built out of dirt, wood, and rocks I found in the backyard. "That's so wonderful," I would hear. "Bravo," "You're so smart and talented," "Why don't you create this...that," and so much more. I also had child-like question and answer sessions. "Why are you different?" I would ask. "Why are you floating around? Can't you walk? Where is your home? Do you have a mother and a father or any brothers and sisters? How long are you going to be around here? Why do I see you but only hear the others? Are they hiding? How come we are friends? Why can't you play with me?" This must have been very entertaining to them, because I remember them engaging in polite laughter at my inquisitiveness.

Beyond play, the Angels were always there for me. I remember one day in particular being frightened by a thunderstorm. The windows trembled from the strong winds and thunder, and the house echoed from creaking noises. Through all of this though, I heard my friendly

Angel tell me in a very loving tone, "Don't worry Peter. There is nothing to be afraid of. It's just very loud rain. Go back to sleep."

No matter what uncomfortable situation I found myself in, I would always get a sense of calm and peace when the Angels were around. I felt loved while in their company, and in later years, I would feel protected. As a youngster I used their soothing voices to lull me to sleep...and sleep I did! To this day, I can still recall the soothing heavenly sound of the Angels' voices in my head.

Run, Run, Run as fast as I can!

As I got older, my need for protection became more persistent. One threatening occasion comes to mind of my parents hiring a mosaic stone worker named Mr. Nick to redo the floors in our house. Mr. Nick was friendly at first, but grew weary of my presence and constant queries. Instead of just ignoring me though, he used the loud roaring noise from the grinding machine and frequent phone breaks to drown me out. As a typical, inner-directed child, I didn't take into consideration that he was trying to do his work. Instead, I took offense and tried even harder to get his attention! The more questions I asked, the more phone breaks he took and the more he ignored me. I found that offensive, so on the third day I decided to tell my father. He found my observations interesting and wanted to know who Mr. Nick called and what he was saying. I couldn't imagine why that was important but the gossip seemed to excite my father, so I was happy to engage in it.

Next morning, after everyone left for work, the doorbell rang. Still in bed, I jumped out to run to the door. It was Mr. Nick. I barely uttered the words, "Good Morning," when his diatribe started. "You son of a bitch, you told of my phone calls? Now I am going to kill you, you little bastard, you have ruined my life! I can't go back home because of you! I'm the laughing stock in the whole neighborhood! I'm going to kill you,

you bastard!" Upon hearing this, I start running in a full sprint to get away from the madman. He bolted in and started chasing me around the house, screaming as he ran. Thoughts were coming to me from the previous night's discussion with my father. 'All this,' I said to myself, 'because I told of his gushy love talk with Mr. So and So's wife?' But in my childlike innocence, I didn't realize the magnitude of what I was implying.

As I darted around every table curve, I realized my life was in extreme jeopardy if this madman were to catch up with me. A few times he'd stop to quickly change direction, trying to catch me coming the other way. Lucky for me he was unsuccessful. At every juncture, he was only one breath and an arm's stretch away from my fleeting body. At one point, he stopped, and I followed suit. I could sense he was up to something, and thought, 'What now?' but in that instant, I had a premonition. A picture of him tightly gripping my throat flashed before me. Already breathless from running and overwrought by fear, I became numb and motionless. After pushing chairs out of the way, he swiftly jumped on the table and closed the gap between us. Then out of no where, and only a split second before he lunged toward me, I saw two ethereal hands grab him by the ankles, causing him to land flat on his belly across the table.

Completely startled, Mr. Nick stopped his pursuit, giving me time to escape. With wings on my legs, I fled the house and headed toward the safety of the nearest hill. I would stay there hidden all day until my father came home, wondering the entire time if I should tell of Mr. Nick's tirade. Later on, when I did retell of the event, it gave everyone a good chuckle, even though I insisted I was almost killed! Father finally said he would go to Nick's house later that evening, but I pleaded for him not to. "Please don't say anything! If you do he is going to come around looking for me all over again tomorrow!" Father went anyway, and that night, sleep was futile. The next day, I begged for someone to stay home with me. Father assured me Mr. Nick would never come around again, but the fear didn't leave my body. Even thinking of my Angel friends couldn't bring me comfort. I wondered, "Would they be able to protect me again?"

That morning the house was on lockdown. Peering through a crack in the front window and another from the back door, I became the look-out for the killer mason. He never did show up that day. The talk father had with him went well and what a relief. Months later, we would run into each other, or should I say, he almost ran into me! I was walking home not realizing that a massive, slow-moving truck was following me. It was Mr. Nick! Unsure if he was going to run me over or not, he honked his crazy loud horn, and I jumped like a frightened cat. He stuck his angry head out the window, screaming, "Ah re baghasa!" Meaning, "You little rascal!" I start screaming back, "I'm going to tell my father later when he gets home!" Without looking back, I tore ahead, full speed through an open field and hid in a familiar hiding spot. Once again, I found myself waiting in terror till the coast was clear. I couldn't help but recall how the Angel reached out to grab him that morning in the kitchen, saving me from a horrible beating. To this day, in fact, I can recall the image of the mason's hands on my throat. And that wasn't the last time the Angel would intervene on my behalf. There was more to come...much more.

We are Not Alone

When we are conscious enough to distinguish that we are surround-ed by ethereal beings, there comes an enormous appreciation. We all have ordinary means of help, but there is extraordinary help as well. Even if help is not obvious from a young age or readily accepted, even-tually it becomes evident as it appears again and again in moments of great need. Simply said, we are not alone. Even in isolation one is not alone. Throughout the years, many of us have heard stories of divine presence and how Angels assisted people while in grave danger. (Who doesn't recall the miraculous landing of the plane on the Hudson River and believe that the pilot wasn't inspired in some profound and divine way?) In any case, getting help from the Angels resonates with me. I believe that's what they do—watch over us.

My intuition tells me that I would not be around today if not for my Angels. This is my truth from childhood up until now. I don't remember how many times over the years I stopped myself from going forward on a green signal because a voice told me to. Each time proved beneficial too as a car would speed by and nearly miss me. Just recently while at a light about to make a left turn, I heard a loud voice in my head telling me to wait. Although I didn't visually see a threat, I listened and stopped. The driver behind me was annoyed about my slow approach to the turn, but his constant beeping didn't affect my caution. Seconds later, a piece of concrete came crashing in front of us from the overpass above.

This type of interaction with the Angels is 'old hat' for me, but nonetheless it is still always exciting and often dramatic! I am very thankful to God and the Angels for looking out for me throughout the years. I thank God for creating the Angels! What an awesome way God shows love for us.

A New Teacher Awaits Approval

Back to Greece and my childhood years, I am trying to remember how the Angels looked and have to admit I don't really remember seeing wings. I do remember them flowing with long, wavy hair and surrounded by beautiful multicolored lights. For the first couple of years, things were normal at times and bizarre at others. Although back then, I wasn't sophisticated enough to know the difference. Somewhere around the age of 5, one of those bizarre events occurred. It started out ordinary, but I sensed something was up after hearing more voices than usual. It seemed they were having discussions about me. One

Angel in particular was getting my attention with some specific questions. "Did you tell him yet?" "Why is he taking so long?" "When are you going to tell him?" My Angel friend's response was, "No, not yet. He's not ready. We need more time." Initially, I wasn't interested in the Q and A session, not until the questioning became repetitive. Eventually, I felt I was letting my friend down for not being ready. I finally got the courage to ask, "Tell me what?" "Oh nothing," the Angel answered, but the exchange about my readiness continued and my curiosity peaked. When the other Angels left, I anxiously asked my friend, "What do they want? Why aren't I ready?" My tone was firm and demanding. "What's wrong?"

There was silence for a moment or two. I assume that I was being assessed, and in a very loving tone, my Angel friend said to me, "They want to know if you are interested in meeting someone who wants to teach you." I quickly responded. "Teach me?" I queried. "What does that mean?"

My friend continued, "He wants to talk with you and show you some things." "No," I replied. "Thank you. I can talk with you. I don't want another friend." Looking back, I imagine I didn't like the idea of someone else teaching me or perhaps I didn't understand what the word "teaching" meant. 'Would my Angel leave me and be replaced?' Regardless, I must have based my decision on how I felt and said, "No." At that point, I was just relieved I hadn't done anything wrong.

From that point on, every time the other Angels came around asking my special friend if I was ready, I would answer for him with a loud, "No!" and off they'd go. They were very persistent though. I often wondered if they were mad at me for refusing, but my loyal Angel would read my thoughts and assure me they were only hanging around in case I changed my mind. "That's all," my Angel friend would say. "Don't worry about anything else." More at ease I would answer, "That's good to know. Thank you!" Eventually, I got tired of them asking over and over again, or maybe just more curious about the teacher who wanted to teach me. I'm not sure how it happened, but eventually I committed to the teachings.

"The Creator placed intelligence in soul, and soul in body, so that His creation would be the fairest and best."

—TIMAEUS OF LOCRI

My Teacher

"Hi, Peter, how are you today? My name is So-and-So, and I'm going to be your teacher." That would have been a nice intro. Instead I got, "Oh so little time and so much to learn," or something like that. This teacher's unimpressive entry didn't compel me to listen. "Excuse me for a second please. Hello...Angels? I don't think I want to learn anything right now!" A little too late for that though, because I was already in agreement with them and had no way out.

Day by day, I was beholden to the teacher and the teachings were getting more frequent, lengthy, and very boring. Imagine the transition of a five-year-old kid who was worry-free at play and keeping company with beautiful Angels to then enter into daily interactions with a tutor who wanted to teach all kinds of strange things. And keep in mind, I didn't have the slightest idea why. What was I, a kid, supposed to do with all that? The teacher seemed different with an unusual appearance. He didn't look like the Angels or anyone I had ever seen before. At that age, I didn't know what Asians looked like, but as I look back I can describe him as such. He was old, average height and slim physique, which was covered by a maroon colored robe. I never saw him smile, but his thin gray mustache and goatee constantly moved while he talked. He would sometimes ask if I was paying attention, but that was only after he tapped me on the shoulder with his stick. I always replied, "Yes," but most of the time, I was not.

After his arrival, life changed drastically. When it was only me and the Angels, interactions were fun, comfortable, effortless, and very spontaneous. After the teacher arrived, I was constantly disciplined. I needed to listen without interrupting, which was not an easy task for one so young. Sometimes he would interrupt my play time in order to teach me. On occasion, the Angels would check in and let me know how proud they were of my behavior. I would ask them when the teaching would be over, lamenting how tiring and boring it was. "Soon," they would say, except soon wasn't soon enough.

For some reason the lessons transpired while sitting on a huge rock. I was out of body, meaning, I was in a dream like state, and because there was so much the teacher thought I needed to know (as he said there was "too much to learn in very little time"), they were done on a consistent and persistent basis. For many years, I had no recollection of becoming any smarter for the efforts either! I remembered more of the daily routine he put me through than the actual knowledge he expressed. I was a kid who wanted to play. The Asian man seemed way too serious.

A curious child, though, I always had lots and lots of questions to ask. I never did get any answers back. It seemed that listening was more important to the teacher. "One day you'll understand" was his normal response. "But I want to know now," I'd say and am still saying to this day! The teachings continued until I was about seven. When I started regular school, all the interactions came to a stop. I don't remember a graduation celebration either. Perhaps the learning is still ongoing? In any case, the Angels must have been relieved considering the frequent requests I made to end the sessions. I considered it a blessing from God when they finally did stop! The Asian teacher had been with me for over two years, and I am surprised I never told anyone, not even my parents. Perhaps I thought all little boys learned that way. Although I never did find out where he came from, many years later these lessons did bear fruit. That was when I finally understood the reason why the Angels brought him to me.

"The vision that you glorify in your mind, the ideal that you enthrone in your heart, this you will build your life by, and this you will become."

—James Allen

It Doesn't Get Any Better

My Angel and my Guide interactions were toned down a bit right after I started going to regular school. I didn't have a clue why, but I wasn't complaining either. Unfortunately, it went without saying that I wasn't happy about meeting my real life teacher at school. I already had an impression that learning wasn't much fun, and for the first few months, I would cry every morning for about an hour before my parents would either convince me, bribe me, or drag me kicking and screaming to go to school. I still remember my very first day. I was only sitting at my desk a few minutes when I felt the need to grab my schoolbag and bolt out. On a fast pace toward the exit and desperately reaching for the doorknob, I heard a voice calling my name. In an unnerving voice I heard the teacher say, "Where are you going, Peter?" "Home," I whispered with tears burgeoning. "You can't go home yet," she stated in a strict tone. "Go back to your seat! I will have none of that in my classroom."

I didn't like her. I didn't like school or my life...the way life was turning out anyway. The new daily routine was different from what I was used to. Not much of a morning person, I liked to get up when I was done sleeping. And being in the same room for most of the day was very claustrophobic. Although the Asian prepped me for learning, I wasn't really prepared for the stringent school experience. Before attending, I was in a comfortable, safe and loving place. Now I was exposed to an unfamiliar, uncomfortable and scary environment.

It seemed that all the other kids weren't happy either, and they demonstrated that by misbehaving. The teacher yelled at us constantly. And to make matters worse, I was learning things that seemed unrelated to the reality I lived up until that point. Lots of thoughts were circulating in my head while observing the class. I felt out of place and different considering everyone's silly behavior. Having had instruction up until that point by my ethereal teacher, the classroom scenario seemed chaotic. Gradually though, I managed to blend in with the kids and adjusted to the routine. I got up every morning without putting up a fight, and once this surrender took place, positive aspects became evident. Having friends that weren't Angels was a new welcomed experience. Playing with other kids and being included in games was exciting as well. By the end of the first year, I transitioned into a fairly good student with an average grade of 9 (10 being the highest). After being given our grades and assignments for the summer, off we went. Free again! My friends and I decided to run some summer contests: Who is going to eat the most ice cream? Who will go on the best vacation? Who will score the most soccer goals?

Summers in Greece were usually wonderful, but I allowed peer pressure and competition to drive myself and my family crazy. And they didn't take anything I said about the contests seriously no matter how I pleaded with them. I so desperately wanted to win the vacation competition and was angered when no one wanted to leave Athens to go somewhere exotic, like to a mountain village or an island. I would bellow at my parents, "That's what everyone else is doing!"

That first summer was disappointing and stressful, and when the time came to go back to school, the crying started all over again.

Not much had changed. The teacher was the same although the class work was more difficult and home assignments more frequent. Thankfully, I maintained the same grades and joined the school chorus. By the third year, everyday homework consisted of spelling, math, history, religion, essays, geography, science, lots of reading, and some new subjects such as poetry. Our days were filled with tons of schoolwork—so much so that there weren't enough hours in the day to finish them.

My First Download

In Greece, back in the late '60s, early '70s, teachers were allowed to physically and mentally discipline kids. Slapping, screaming, and getting hit on one's hands with the ruler or getting one's ears pulled were routine disciplinary actions for incomplete assignments. As I look back at my school experience, I can liken it to boot camp with a lot of yelling and long hours, six days a week. At times I really think the teachers enjoyed using the rulers and olive branches to hurt us. There was one day that I was loaded with homework, and one assignment in particular was stressing me out. I needed to copy a page of calligraphy, and my attempts went late into the night and past my bedtime. I was getting a little desperate, but there was no one up that late to help me. Even though thoughts of being hit with the ruler ran rampant in my head, I started to put my pencils and notebook away. Suddenly, I was reminded of my friends. I hadn't interacted with the Angels for a while, but I was recalling the numerous times they had helped me. Not knowing exactly what they could do to help now, or even if they could hear my plea, I asked anyway. "Angels," I said with my mind, "please help me." As soon as the words left my head, I felt their presence. A familiar sense of joy and love overwhelmed me.

"Hi, Peter," my Angel friend said. "How are you?" "Hi," I answered back. "I'm not doing that good, and tomorrow I'm going to get hit by the teacher because I can't do my calligraphy assignment." "Don't worry,

Peter," The Angel stated. "Take out your pencils and notebook and try again." I argued, "But I've being trying all night, and I'm very bad at calligraphy." The Angel reassured me. "It will be easier for you now." I was hoping I would hear, 'No problem, I'll do the calligraphy for you!' Instead, I listened by getting out my notebook, turning to a new page, and with a new sharpened pencil, I started to write. The lead was touching the page, but doubts were running through my head. 'Why don't they try themselves? I already know that I can't do it. What's the point?' My thoughts were suddenly interrupted. "Look at the first letter and concentrate, Peter," the Angel said. I forgot for the moment that they could hear my thoughts! "Yes, I am looking," I said discouraged, and then started to write. To my surprise, my hand was moving on its own in a soft, curving motion with perfect precision. The first letter came out looking magical as well as every one after. My rendition looked even better than the handout sheet!

Drawing became effortless, simple and natural. I wondered if the Angels were taking over my hand. 'Who cares! My homework is getting done!' The best part was the release of anxiety and fear of being beaten the next day. I had reason to smile. My hand continued to move at a pretty fast pace and within a short time, the whole page was perfectly done and amazing. "Yes, Peter, you see?" The Angel complimented me. "You did great!" And great it was. The more I looked at what I had done, the happier I became. I truly felt proud of myself. I don't remember if I gave my gratitude and all the credit to the Angels at the time. Hopefully I did. I was blown away by the experience and somewhat confused, not understanding how 'channelling' worked. The next morning, I was trying to tell my family what had taken place by waving my masterpiece around, but they were too busy eating breakfast to pay any attention. It didn't really bother me though. I was used to being ignored by family members. It was my teacher that I was most excited to show my beautiful calligraphy to. 'She will be so proud of me,' I thought. That was the very first time I was actually happy and looking forward to going to school. I considered it a great morning!

After arriving at school, I excitedly handed in my homework assignments. It was midday after lunch break when the teacher asked to see me. I started questioning myself, 'Is she going to show everyone in class my beautiful work? Wow what an honor!' Getting closer to her desk, I saw my notebook in her hand so I continued to think my moment of glory was approaching. That thought changed quickly though the minute she opened her mouth. "Peter," she exclaimed, "how dare you! In my classroom you hand in a homework assignment that was done by your parents?" My mouth suddenly dropped to the floor. "What?" I said astounded. "But...but..." and that was all that I could say before the great honors* started. She was furious and came at me with the ruler, using it with a vicious vengeance.

I don't remember much of what else happened that day or what other consequences ensued due to what she considered my wrongful behavior. The standard procedure in cases like this one was a note to the parents. Through the years, I've asked my mother and the family about that day, but no one recalled specifically. In general when the teacher or the school principal asked for my parents, they would send my older brother in their place since they both worked. The incident must have affected me a lot, because months later I came to the conclusion that school wasn't all that important anymore and definitely wasn't for me. 'Why bother? I'm out of here.'

Peter on the Mountain

One day I just decided it was time for school days to come to an end, so I created a master plan. I got up in the morning, got ready, and just like every other school day, I headed out in the same direction. A short distance down the road, though, I took a turn toward the mountains. I thought everything through. Well, almost everything.

---

* Honors: In Greece the word "honors" was used to describe getting beaten with an olive branch. The term came from the practice of throwing olive branches at champion runners.

There were a few issues that needed to be addressed. Because I didn't have a watch, I didn't know what time to go back home. I had to climb to the highest point of the mountain so I could see another school in the area. Luckily all schools finished at the same time, so when they released the students, I headed back home. When I was hungry, I would take the back trails into a nearby town to buy lunch. It was a long walk but a necessary safety net, since I didn't know anyone in the other neighborhood, and they didn't know me. Although I did get caught once by a grocery store owner. "Why are you not in school?" he asked, "Ah…I didn't have school today!" I lied, and he knew I was lying, so I grabbed the food and ran out of his store. Not able to go back there again, I had to rotate between different stores not to raise further suspicion.

It was scary staying all day at the mountain with its many noises and other inconveniences, but the thought of school and the teacher was scarier, so I adjusted to the fear of being alone. In doing so, I made some new friends…mostly birds and squirrels that I shared my lunch with. Lucky for me I never had to fight off a fox or stray dog. Everything went smoothly for the first two weeks. Since I was inventing the homework assignments, I made them short and very easy, but after realizing no one was checking them anyway, I decided reading was easier to pretend to do. Occasionally, I would be asked if I finished all of my homework and studying. "Of course," I would avow. "I did it!"

Except for missing my friends, I enjoyed almost every moment I was away from school. Life was good, and as a nine year old, I didn't foresee any problems like report cards that would arrive or the possibility that the teacher or school principal would start looking for me. Instead, I thought about how much fun it would be to have others join me. I decided to share the secret with a few of my closest friends. I couldn't wait for the next morning and of my secret telling. Just thinking about it filled me with happiness. I was thrilled to execute this aspect of my great plan.

Unfortunately, later that day an unexpected event would ruin everything. Alexandra, the girl who lived next door, showed up at my house. "Peter are you in there? Hello . . . ?" She asked, "Peter, open the door." I was annoyed and wondered why she was looking for me and what she wanted. "Leave me alone." I whispered to myself. Hoping she would go away, I stayed put, but she just kept coming back every ten minutes or so. I escaped out of the back door and found a hiding spot in the yard where I could keep an eye on her. She sat and waited trying to catch me going in or out of the house. I was on to her antics and waited it out. Unfortunately, neither of us would budge until my mother came home. I watched in a cold sweat as mom opened the gate and walked right passed my hiding spot. Alexandra spoke up. "Hello," she said to my mother. "Is Peter sick or something, because he hasn't been in school for a while and the teacher sent me looking for him." At first, my mother thought the eight year old was just playing, so she started calling my name. Alexandra stopped her though. "He's not home," she said. "I've been calling him for an hour."

That statement seriously scared me! The plan was ruined, and I felt the need to escape. Staying out of sight, I waited for the right moment and took off toward the mountain once again. This time though, I was escaping my mother's and father's honors. All afternoon and into the night, I sat on the mountain. It was darker and scarier than during the day, but not having an option, I stayed and waited for things to cool off. It wasn't long before I was able to hear voices of friends and neighbors looking for me. The embarrassment was too much to for me to handle though so I sought refuge deep in the forest.

Sitting alone in the dark there was plenty of time to run the different scenarios in my head. I optioned the harsh punishment and humiliation with all the other potential consequences of being in the woods (with the wolves) and without food. Eventually I went home to take the punishment, but not right away. I waited until everyone was asleep. When I finally did head down, the immediate area was quiet and there were only a few houses lit up. As I approached my yard, I heard my mother calling my name. I stayed close and hid behind a tree. Every ten minutes or so she came out, walked the 200 feet to the end of the property and anxiously called again. I felt bad about the concerned tone in her voice and finally yelled back. "I'm okay, but I'm not going back home!" I caught sight of my siblings and didn't want them to come after me so I started to take off. My mother shouted back, "Just come home. No one is going to touch you." I didn't believe her. "Yeah, right!" I yelled and tried to run faster, but when I realized I had no where to run, I just stood frozen. My older brother saw my state of fear and took advantage of it by telling me stories of all the monsters in the woods. He was finally able to grab me by the arm, but at that point, I conceded knowing there were no other options. On the way back down the hill, I remember looking up at the bright moon surrounded by all the glistening stars and wished I was up there with them.

Punishment Takes A Turn

Unfortunately, my view of the stars in the sky were replaced by stars in my head. I got the dreaded whipping I deserved for all the trouble I caused. Next morning, my brother escorted me to school to make sure I arrived and to talk with my teacher. Part two of my rightfully due punishment was there waiting for me, but first I would have to endure some further torture from my brother. By the time we arrived, I was a wreck and ready to faint from fear. He led me in with a good grip on my arm, but not because he thought I might escape. It was because my legs were too weak to walk! The classroom was on the second floor, and he had to partially carry me. A few steps before opening the door, he told me, "Don't say anything, just listen and look sick." That was easy! "But I am sick," I muttered. "Just keep your mouth shut," he told me. "Ok," I mumbled back.

He knocked on the door, waited for a reply, and together we entered. "Good morning, I'm Peter's brother, and I had to bring him to school today being that you have asked for him. Although he's much better now, he's still very weak from his recent illness." My eyes were wide from shock as I looked at him. He continued, "He's still a little out of it because of the medication and all, but we heard you're looking for him, so we fixed him up, and here he is." Every kid in the class looked at me. The teacher was totally taken by surprise, and by the look on her face, I could tell she was reluctant to welcome me back. Thinking quickly, I started moaning. She sized us both up and finally said, "Why don't you take him back home for today. It is fine for Peter to come back when he feels better." We hightailed it out of there and laughed all the way back home. Many years later, I asked him about that morning and his rescue. It turns out that it wasn't his idea after all. Afraid of the beating and the backlash I would have to endure, my parents had him tell the tall tale. That day, I was happy to learn that Angels came in many forms.

Is This Friend Really Imaginary?

Even if there is no direct contact or known interaction with them, Angels are always there to protect and help us, sometimes even working through people we interact with. We also have our own unique gifts that we bring to share for the sake of our own growth in life. It helps when there's support early on, and it is great when the family understands, recognizes, and assists. After all, they are our very first teachers. And if they don't, that's OK too, as long as they do no harm. Parents are either inspired by or afraid of the behavior their out-of-the-ordinary kids exhibit. In my opinion, it all varies on the awareness they each have. I didn't feel safe in my younger years talking to my parents (or anyone for that matter) about my experiences. I have, though, heard many stories from other children throughout the years who had imaginary friends or deceased family members they interacted with. Except for a very few, most parents were uncomfortable and decidedly not proud of their kids for having this ability. I'm without judgment of these parents realizing how inexplicably strange and scary it may seem to most.

Alice Didn't Stay in Wonderland

Alice was about three when conversations with her imaginary playmate started. Although they deemed it cute, her parents didn't render it important at first. It became more serious to them after they finally asked Alice who the friend was. Alice responded by pointing to a picture on the wall of her grandmother. Her mother was astonished and frightened. She immediately took Alice to a specialist to test her sanity. After being told Alice was fine, both parents tried to ignore the interactions she had with her grandmother. For the most part, it became a hidden and well-kept secret within the immediate family. When the interactions finally ended, the family was relieved. Thirty years later, one of those family members asked Alice if she remembered speaking with her dead grandmother, but she had no recollection. Realizing there was more to learn, she came to me for a healing session. I wasn't surprised at all when we brought back the memories through hypnosis.

"If you want your children to be intelligent, read them fairy tales."

—Albert Einstein

Gifts Come in Different Ways

We all have abilities and talents, but the means we come to realize these abilities may vary greatly due to acceptance. Spiritual gifts are hard for ordinary thinkers to accept. If you think about it, we readily acknowledge and accept high IQ's, amazing vocal and dramatic capabilities, sports and all sorts of human talent much easier than spiritual aptitude. We are impressed. We admire and enjoy. We are in gratitude and amazement of all of the magnificently expressed talents and creativity there is in this world. More importantly, there is an innate understanding of their possible origin that doesn't need any explanation. All we really care about talent is how it makes us feel as it awes, uplifts and overwhelm us. It is this spark we get from creative and gifted people that ignites our own inspiration and allows us to connect back to source... the place we feel whole and fulfilled. Spiritual gifts can and will do the same, but not without acceptance.

As a young boy, I met a gifted person whose spark left a lifelong impression within me. While playing by the front yard, I amused myself with a game I called, "Spying on the Enemy," which was inspired by the military presence that was stationed in our neighborhood. Camouflaged in dirt and leaves, my plan was to get close enough to observe the enemy. I crawled on my elbows through bushes, approaching the enemy army truck at their post. My first tactic was to go unseen. I stayed put for a while in silence and spied on two chatty soldiers standing near their truck. The mission was going great, and I managed to get close enough to hear what they were saying without being noticed. Actually, they had no clue. Not being satisfied with the ease of this game though, I decided to surprise them by coming out of hiding and demanding their surrender.

My plan worked...sort of. While squirming through plants and shrubs to get to them, something sharp got in my left eye. I came out yelling and screaming from pain, scaring the hell out of them! Being so startled from my antics, both reached for their weapons...one pointing his machine gun at me while the other a pistol! Luckily, the pistol holder recognized me as a child with an injury and pushed down his partner's machine gun before any harm was done. "My eye! My eye!" I screamed in agony while running away in circles desperately crying out, "Help me! My eye!"

The noise engaged the whole neighborhood. Curious, they quickly came out and after getting a look, came to my rescue. I couldn't stand still from the pain, so I ran in circles. It felt like someone was ripping my eye out. Patia, a grandmother-like figure and neighbor from next door, was the first to come to the rescue. "Peter, let me see your eye." My eye was hurting too much for me to stop the ranting. "Let me see, Peter!" she yelled while chasing behind me. Eventually, the two soldiers caught me and kept my body still while she investigated. She took her left thumb and forefinger and started making the sign of the cross on my lid, rubbing up and down and side to side. After a few whispered prayers, she stopped, and in an instant the sharp pain was gone! Looking back now, I can claim that my eye wasn't even irritated. "You feel better?" she asked. "How's your eye? Is it OK now? Open your eye. Don't be afraid. You can see?"

God bless her soul. 'Grandma' Patia was a great lady. She helped so many people over the years with her gifts. She even rescued my brother once from choking on an apple. He was turning blue by the time she got to him, but she dug her finger down his throat and picked that apple right out of him. The situation was terrifying, but she was amazing to watch! She also knew so much about herbs and healing remedies. After falling and tearing my knee open, she applied a cream and tied an onion on my leg. Before the remedy, I was in pain and couldn't sleep; it was taking forever to heal. Magically the cream-and-onion combo took away the pain and helped to speed up the healing process. I still have the scar, but am deeply appreciative of her gift of healing. Patia was the type of person that you were always glad to see. And when one happened to cross paths with her, she would always have a big smile on her face and a loving blessing for you; "Peter, may God be always with you!"

Mr. Vlahos and His Gift

This area of Greece seemed to be a magical place. There were many others with gifts and skills that lived there, such us the popular Mr. Vlahos. His gift was fixing broken bones. I personally had never met him (he was before my time), but I heard many great stories. People loved and admired him, but not all were happy about him practicing his gift. One day, Mr. Vlahos was taken to court for practicing medicine without the proper qualifications. Many of his supporters came out the day of his trial. Among them, were those who had been healed or helped or knew of someone who was. Some were in need at the time and wanted to see Mr. Vlahos continue to offer his services. For the sake of justice, though, doctors protested and testified against his practice and his lack of medical skills.

Not understanding what an attorney was, Mr. Vlahos was not represented. When asked if he had someone there to speak for him, a little puzzled Mr Vlahos said, "Why would I need someone else to speak for me if I'm already here?" When asked what he had to say in his own defense, he responded, "Your Honor, I'm not an educated man, but if I am allowed, I would like to bring into the courtroom my sheep that's tied up outside to help me explain." His statements caused outbreaks of laughter, but as preposterous as it sounded, the judge allowed his request. Mr. Vlahos gladly went to fetch his four-legged legal adviser.

When he returned, he stood with his sheep in front of the judge and asked if he could address the expert doctors. Again, the judge allowed the man his request. Mr. Vlahos looked directly at the doctors and asked, "All of you sitting over there are trained doctors and experts that fix broken bones, aren't you?" "Yes," they replied. "If so, then can you fix this?" He grabbed the sheep's front leg and snapped it, audibly breaking the bone. Everyone in the courtroom was stunned, most especially the poor little sheep! He then picked up the sheep and walked over toward the shaken doctors. He asked them again to fix the sheep's leg. "You are experts, aren't you? You can fix broken bones, right? Well, there is a broken bone right in front of you. Why don't you practice your medicine and fix its leg?" Outraged, their defense team rose. "Your Honor," they exclaimed. "This is preposterous! Never have we encountered such outrageous behavior in a courtroom!" Not knowing what else to say, they continued insulting Mr. Vlahos. "Obviously proper court behavior as well as medical intelligence is nonexistent in this defendant." The doctors chimed in, "We can't position the leg back in its place without the tools, equipment, and the right setting. Your Honor, we refuse to do it here, but if we have to, we can bring the sheep to our offices and proceed properly."

Mr. Vlahos wasn't settling. He retorted by requesting His Honor to demand they fix the "poor sheep's broken leg" right there for all to witness. The judge went along with the request and again asked the doctors, "Well, can you?" "No, Your Honor," they responded. Mr. Vlahos turned his attention back to the judge. "Your Honor, God has given me this gift...more of a necessity, I guess, as I am a shepherd by trade. These little devils run and climb and sometimes fall and break their limbs. It is such a waste to put them to rest." As he spoke, Mr. Vlahos started manipulating the sheep's leg. "Throughout the years," he continued, "people heard of my gift and have asked me to help with their animals' broken limbs and sometimes with their own." As he finished his statement, he lowered the sheep to the ground. Sure enough, it stood on its own and scampered out of the courtroom. The case was immediately closed.

Are We All Gifted?

Let's assume for just a moment that we all have some psychic abilities. In its greatest form, we will call it knowingness and prophecy and to a lesser degree, intuition and perception. Just considering the concept of another sense would suggest that this other dimension of thinking would allow all of us to experience life differently. I began to wonder if there is a time when we all know for certain that we are gifted with vibrant senses. Do we all have them at birth and then slowly lose them? If so, how were they lost? Why do some gain in strength and awareness? It is my guess that it has to do with the amount of support we get from our parents, peers and other people of influence.

After speaking with gifted individuals, much of their growth or lack thereof was due to the initial reaction they received from their loved ones. Without support, these people shut down, discouraged by being different, most especially if the gifts were thought of as negative. Age plays a role as well. When young, we can't make an accurate assessment of what we are dealing with. I can't emphasize enough to parents how influential all closely related adults are in their child's development. Every one of influence needs to be aware and well informed about the child's gift in order to support them. We are so perceptive about giving and receiving love at a young age, so it is important to give only supportive and loving reactions. Anything less is detrimental, lending itself to separation, detachment and adult alienation. The love and acceptance from family will influence a child's desire to hold onto a "gift" they don't necessarily understand. Often times, these special people, for the sake of self perseverance and the comfort of others, instinctively choose to blend in. Any remnant of resonating fear can lead to a space of discord and act as a block to awareness, intuition, perception, and psychic abilities. This will prevent a gifted person from seeing truth about themselves and hinder their potential to become more empowered.

The Pants Pocket

Anita was five and very intuitive. Her psychic abilities were wide and open to maximum capacity. One morning, a commotion outside her room woke her. Being a curious kid, she went to investigate. Her mother and father were frantically searching for his wallet, apparently lost from the night before. "Mommy, Mommy," Anita yelled as she raced to the laundry room, "I know where the wallet is!" After sorting through some clothes in the basket on the floor, Anita finds the wallet in exactly the place she saw it in her head...the pocket of her father's pants.

She happily ran toward her parents, waving the wallet and proudly yelling, "I found the wallet. I found it!" Both parents, stressed and confused asked her, "How did you know the wallet was there?" "I saw where it was in my head," Anita said. Both parents, unhappy with the answer, continued to ask if she had hidden it there. More questions ensued and the child became despondent, not understanding why her parents weren't happy. Her moment of triumph became the moment she shut her gift down. And who could blame her?

Support: The Deciding Factor

There is no blame here, but there is a level of comfort or discomfort that is created each time a child, or any gifted person for that matter, use their paranormal gifts, and it is based on other people's perception. The younger the person, the more impressionable (s)he is. Later in life when there is deeper understanding and consciousness, a better distinction about the appropriate ways and times to apply and talk about these gifts is formed.

It was fear that became the greatest factor in almost ending my desire to utilize my gifts after being punished and beaten for my excellence (obtained by my Angels) in calligraphy. I can't imagine how much worse the outcome would have been if I told anyone that Angels helped me! And I can imagine explaining the Asian teacher or any of the out-of-body experiences...knowing my family, I would have been led to a psychiatric lock up for sure.

Whether we shut down and isolate or gradually allow the gifts to fade, most gifted people have the instinctive need to fit in and go unnoticed. No one wants to appear crazy. No one wants to be beaten with a ruler for perfect calligraphy either! Most of my childhood could not be considered positive, even if it turned out for my own good. I didn't feel protected from adult ridicule, and much of it registered as punishment. After being beaten, it took a very long time to ask for angelic assistance again. Not only did I not dare to ask for it, I also made sure to forget everything that I experienced. Maybe that was the plan all along. They were protecting me from a straitjacket. Everyone played their role, I guess. I accept that, and put it all on karma. It was what it may have needed to be.

I learned from this that all people who are in a position to teach children have a huge responsibility to inspire and help each child discover their unique spark. Socrates, along with many others, were great examples of this by teaching their students how to think, not what to think. It's important for the sake of human evolution to nurture evolving spirits into a world where they can be embodied and supported for who they are. Craving knowledge and advancement is an important task for humanity, and it is equally important for every individual to seek self growth.

Our struggle is to achieve an era of human advancement and spiritual awakening...a solution to end all fears and fear-based human limitations. Although my curiosity was diminished early on by adult ridicule, wonderment that comes from learning resurfaced again in my teens. At seventeen, I wanted to know something about everything. I didn't care much about learning anything in school and will assume I held onto some emotional trauma. But I was happy to once more thirst for answers, to research, to discover and to know. I was led to my local library and relished in all sorts of topics ranging from planetary to evolutionary, historic (mostly Hellenic) to philosophical, religious to metaphysical. Even meditation and yoga held my interest.

If I lost interest, I would quickly start looking for something more appealing. Socrates was very intriguing, as well as Hippocrates, Homer, Sophocles, and Pythagoras, to name a few. I was equally fascinated by the stories of Ulysses and of Greek mythology.

Some of what I gleaned like yoga and meditation, I kept for my entire life. At first, I found meditation challenging and became somewhat discouraged. Perhaps if I had a teacher it would have been easier, because my mind was always very busy with thoughts and images. The wonderful sensations it offered kept me interested, though, and my body would often buzz and tingle from indescribable vibrations. When restlessness persisted, so did my desire to try new ways to focus. I kept reading more books and exploring more techniques and postures. The best advice I found was about bringing focus to the breath. After trying it, I realized that each inhale and exhale helped me bring attention to the present moment, and the oxygen that each breath brought in allowed me to feel more calm and relaxed. This was information I would be using my entire life.

A quote by Sophocles (c. 496–406 BCE), Greek poet and tragedy playwright, author of Oedipus and Antigone, found in the three Theban plays by Sophocles, says, *"One word frees us of all the weight and pain of life: The word is love."*

Angels Watching Over

As the years went by, I learned not to share anything out of the ordinary. It wasn't easy taming the need I had to explore and talk about the unexplained episodes of my life. Eventually, it demanded my attention, and I had no choice but to look closer at its roots and dig under the surface. I also wanted desperately to be able to go back to the Angels, but even if I desperately needed it, there was a time in my younger years that I wouldn't even consider asking them again...or God for that matter...for assistance.

Now of course I understand that we can all ask for help, even if we have never had angelic experiences growing up. There is so much help around us at all times that, if ethereal beings had physical bodies we would need to ask them for their share of the rent! When people choose to remain unaware of ethereal beings, they would never understand the willingness there is on their part to help us. Instead people isolate themselves and use their human resources to obtain answers and solutions to problems. Most don't believe they need outside help, thinking their mind is all they need. The mind has all the answers, but are they the *right* answers? The mind shares a view, but can it possibly have the whole picture? Does it clearly show or explain to us, for example, how we got to that place of anguish in the first place?

The mind detects the feelings we radiate with and will accommodate memories that have conditioned us into thinking a certain way. It tries to satisfy our needs and wants at that moment too, regardless of what is necessary for our wholeness or what is factual. In other words, it makes things up as it goes along!

I lived my life no different from any other human, having attachments to people and things irrespective of how good or bad they were for my well being. I acted and reacted to circumstances and took small steps forward with caution, because I was not aware enough to understand the need to ask for ethereal help during any typical life struggle. I coped and dealt with immediate issues the best I could, unaware of how hard I was working to either keep my heart open or to keep it closed. I believe when people are shutting down for any reason, it's easier to isolate their feelings and their hearts than it is to find the courage to speak the truth and face the consequences. And this was no different for me. Not only did I refuse to open my eyes, I created a shield that kept me out of the Angel Realm.

A full shutdown of the heart has a domino effect. It shuts one's intuitive (right) mind, it changes one's energy which can attract other close-hearted and close-minded people. It allows for all the ingredients to produce a permanently closed life. As a result, lack of goodness changes one's belief system and justifies and supports a conduct that perpetuates itself! Life can become a roller-coaster of emotional deceptions and allows the close-hearted person to become less than what they would have ever accepted if they were true to themselves and their gifts without reprisal from others.

The sorrow is that divine guidance is always present, even in self in-duced isolation. Angels still exist for us and want to help us always. If the drama in one's life has taken over, Angels are ignored and the intuition blocked. Happily, just because we have blocked the Angels, they still try in subtle ways to help us. Their help is divinely aligned with our life plan and won't exceed our own level of awareness and willingness. This makes sense, since their guidance wouldn't be accepted by us if we can't comprehend it. We wouldn't be able to hear or see potential solutions if they "spoke over our head" as the saying goes.

To analogize, let's create a fictional character named Jim and give him all kinds of drama. Life is hard for Jim and nothing, including relationships, ever seems to work out. When a great opportunity opens up for an Angel to offers valuable wisdom, Jim is not in the space of receiving such help. He can't hear a thing. Thank God that our Angels don't have emotions like us and just give up. Instead, these beautiful beings watch Jim struggle and consistently try to help while he keeps making the same mistakes over and over again. We have all had friends like Jim at one time or another. We saw a way out for them...a way to make their life become easier, but they can't or won't hear advice offered, so their lives just kept getting more challenging. It's frustrating for an advisor to watch this. Even harder to imagine, but we have all been Jim! How often do we say to ourselves, "I should have listened to so and so?" or "I should have gone with my gut?"

Coming to America

There was much that blocked me from angelic advice in the next few years. One that offered the most adjustment was our family's move to New York. I was twelve years old when I was told we were leaving Greece, and it made me happy. Everyone else in the family and neighborhood was upset about it, and I didn't understand their sadness. They would frequently ask me why I was so happy. "Who wouldn't want to go there?" I would respond. Back then, I remember how everyone outside of Greece was looked up to and how every body admired Americans. Going to America would be like a dream come true for most people. The belief was that money was literally found laying on the ground, and all one had to do was pick it up. Listening to these stories, albeit true or not, leaves an impression on a young boy. I wanted to go and pick up some of those dollars to buy new toys. Who wouldn't? I remember one of our neighbors asking me what made me so happy to go. I told him it was because of all the different TV channels I was going to be able to watch like westerns, cartoons and war movies. He couldn't imagine how I knew that.

My father lived in New York alone for three years before he came back to get us. He worked hard during that time so he could provide us with many things we couldn't have if we stayed in Greece. We loved it, but wanted more, and expectations (especially mine) were high. Arriving there was a/ great disappointment. New York was nothing like we'd imagined. Everything from the houses, streets, cars, and the people all looked unusual from my perspective. Even the scent of the air seemed different. It was a huge wake-up call that crushed all the dreams I had envisioned in my head. It was an obvious downgrade considering we moved from a house on a hilly mountainside into an old apartment on a second floor of a two family house in Queens. I felt cheated out of the dream, and there was no improvement in my life. I finally understood why everyone was sad about leaving. I became equally sad.

The biggest of all the adjustments was going to school, and not only because I already hated school, but imagine not speaking the language! Upon arrival in America, I didn't know more than a few words of English like hello, thank you, yes, no, good morning, good evening, and good night. I wasn't prepared for junior high at PS 145 in Jackson Heights. Assigned to a bilingual class, I managed to speak the local language very quickly. Unfortunately, it was not English! Learning Spanish went muy bien. Thankfully, my teacher was nice enough to take the extra time I needed to learn English too. In order to help me understand, she would actually ask Mr. Kostakis, the school security man, to translate for her. Mr. Kostakis had a very Greek name, but his Greek was as poor as my English. In the process of translation, the three of us would seem clueless, and most of the time, I was left that way. As much as I liked the teacher, though, I could not say the same for my classmates. I experienced firsthand how it felt to be an outsider. I learned to cope, but only enjoyed a few classes like gym and lunch. Sad to say, but still lucky for me, as newcomers arrived, they got the attention of the bullies, which took the attention off of me.

High School

The Angels must have protected me through the junior high-school years, because I don't remember anything out of the ordinary occurring. High school was a little crazier, especially the first two years as there were always student fights. Often the fighting got so bad that school buses needed police escorts. I remember needing to be frisked before entering the school and having to take public transportation for our safety. Every week there was something to be concerned about. It seemed students were going to school to create havoc, not to be educated.

In the meantime, I put my interest in meditation and yoga, which kept me busy and out of trouble. When meditating, a lot of thoughts came in...thoughts that I now realize must have been ethereal messages, but the books said specifically not to allow distractions to enter. When I got distracted by images, thoughts and even audible remarks, I would tune into my breathing and everything would quiet down. Quite possibly, these were ongoing teachings by my childhood Guides. Yoga on the other hand, was a different story. It was harder and more physically challenging. Since I wasn't very flexible or in as good physical shape as the people posing in the yoga books, the challenge proved too much for my self esteem. Realizing I was never going to be able to manipulate myself into a pretzel, I lost interest and gave it up. The practice did prove helpful later when I enrolled in Karate class with a friend. I realized how much more flexible I was than the other kids, and surprisingly quick at learning the moves. My instructor must have seen something in me, because he used to push me a little more than the others. He was aware that I was holding back and hesitant to stand out. A shy kid, I didn't make friends easily, nor did I speak much. I kept to myself and never wanted to be the center of attention. I also didn't like to be combative in the one-on-one fights. I'm still surprised I went and have no recollection of why I originally told my friend I would join.

No Will to Fight

The first couple of weeks I had fun learning how to block kicks and punches. That was all fun, but fun turned to dread as soon as I had to apply it. I then learned I wasn't much of a fighter! With some coaching and plenty of black and blues, I got better at blocking. I was swift at defense but never felt comfortable applying my contact skills. It wasn't until I was pushed against the wall, literally, that something super human came over me, and I found myself doing ninja-like things I hadn't even learned in class.

The teacher was impressed. He also caught on that I didn't want to use those contact skills so he pushed me to participate more. While engaged in one-on-one combats, I put in minimum effort, just enough to not call attention to myself. One of those weird ninja moments came while I was fighting a new guy who, for some reason, felt the need to punch and wave his arms like a street fighter. I kept putting myself in a position to hit him but wouldn't swing. The more I did that, the more aggressive he became, but I was quick on my feet. At one point when he lunged forward, I was at his back and able to firmly punch him, but instead I applied a tap. My gentleman-like moves irritated him so much he went after me like a bull goes after a matador. Each time he caught up with me, he did whatever sloppy move he could to inflict pain. I was frustrated he was so un-sportsman like. The teacher got frustrated too and yelled to me in Greek to "Hit him." Instead, I took a defensive pause, and the street fighter came toward me with a vengeance. I took a step in and with the roar of a lion, threw a front punch that had so much force, it stunned both of us! His body folded, hit the floor and eerily slid across the room. It was obvious that there was a strange force behind the punch. It was as if something took over my body and this unknown strength scared me. The street fighter lost his breath and actually had to be assisted out of the room. Later on when I saw him in the locker room, he showed me my fist imprint on his chest. I apologized and told him he pushed me a little too much. "I lost my temper," I told him. He knew it too and never came back again.

The Brick Chopper

Two months later, one of the highest black-belt holders at the time, an eighth degree grand master in Koei-Kan named Grand Master Kaloudis, came to our school to hold an exhibition. I was looking forward to it, but for some reason I didn't arrive on time. Embarrassed, I stood outside the glass door and peaked in. The school was packed, and everyone's gaze was upon the grand master as he spoke. When I finally decided to go in, I tried to slip by unnoticed, but my teacher caught sight of me and motioned for me to get to the locker room and change.

I walked past everyone in fear of being in trouble, quickly changed into my ghi, then snuck back in towards the rear of the room.

I listened as Grand Master Kaloudis spoke about Karate and some of the virtues of martial arts, how good it was for the body, our character, discipline, and clarity of the mind. When he ended his speech, my teacher walked to the center of the floor and they each took a bow of respect towards one another. Announcements of more special events ensued as the black-belted students set up a stack of 5 bricks in front of the Grand Master. We were all excited knowing what was about to happen, and our mouths were held open in anticipation. Grand Master stared at the bricks intently and began to measure his punch, bringing his arm up and down in slow motion. Suddenly without warning and in one swift movement that could barely be deciphered, his hand split the pile of bricks in two! We all gasped and looked at one another realizing that even breaking one brick was intense for the school's black belts to achieve and that was after a few attempts, let alone with one tiny movement!

Grand Master then laid down on his side with only his elbow touching the floor to demonstrate that there was no body force behind the strikes. It was just a slight motion of his hand. There was so much power in this little man with no obvious physical clues to imply this strength either. He moved with shift precision through his routine, continuing to use his iron fist or open palm to slice through more bricks like a knife cuts through butter.

Was it the Angels?

After the Master finished with the bricks, the black belts came back out to show off their skills, but the emotion behind the fighting was too intense for me. Up until that point, I had not witnessed that much aggression at our school. The teacher pointed his finger towards five of my classmates to do a kata demonstration, one of them being the kid right in front of me. That finger point took me by surprise. The thought of possibly being picked made my body heat up like a pot on a stove. Then he randomly picked pairs for one on one combat, and I was off the hook again. Thinking I was safe, I started to relax, but when the final event came, he picked me to fight one of the teaching assistants...a soon-to-be black belt. Totally shaken, my legs barely took me to the center of the floor. I could feel the sensation of eyes boring into the back of my head as I stood opposite Mr. G. That's what we called him.

Our teacher indicated the start. I wasn't ready, but set out to do the best I could. Blocking his kicks and punches while dancing around him, I avoided some of his blows. Nevertheless, Mr. G was kicking my butt. The grand master was observing on the sideline and started yelling encouraging words. There wasn't much to compliment as I was barely applying any technique other than some great escapes. After hearing him, though, courage replaced my fear. I started to feel powerful energy rise up in me. My counter attacks became more fluent, and my body was moving with its own intuition.

After a couple of my bonsai hits, Mr. G had to actually stop to catch his breath. His glare told me he was angry. I couldn't blame him, because by this point, I was trying to be cool by dancing around, faking punches and squarely landing my kicks. I was partially aware of this taunting, but the cheers coming from my classmates were fueling my bravado. He finally dropped any need he thought he had to be a nice guy and started to look at me as his equal...except I wasn't. What started out as a fun demonstration was turning into a match that could be likened to David and Goliath.

I wanted it to be over, but it seemed to be taking forever. As I was looking at the clock, he came at me fast with a round kick. I somehow got behind him and instantly ducked under his leg as if something had moved me out of its reach. Although at the time, I was not aware of an angelic presence, as I look back, I can't imagine how I stayed safe without it. Not wanting to keep going, I wished for an ending. It was then that a clear picture of his next move registered in my mind. It was intuition for sure, and with the ease of a master, I delivered a hard side kick to his midsection before he could hit me. That ended the fight quickly. I wasn't proud of my actions and hoped that he was all right. Shortly after that day, I decided to quit. I never felt comfortable practicing there again.

Karate Wasn't 'The Way'

Just a teen, I couldn't fully grasp what was making me so uncomfortable. At first I thought fear of fighting could be an instigating factor, but that didn't make sense since I had confidence in my ability. It was more about not recognizing myself and what I became when I fought. That was something I didn't want to further investigate. Many years later when I could handle it, I went under hypnosis and was able to reconcile what happened during my Karate experiences. The hypnosis regressed me to another lifetime in Asia where I was invited to demonstrate my fighting skills at a martial arts school. Apparently, I was pretty good back then too!

Karate was a way for me to learn self defense, which was necessary during my high school years, and most likely, that was the primary reason I took classes. I realize now, though, that I might have been energetically and unconsciously attracting all of these challenging situations. It was as if I had the need to be punished and put on the spot consistently throughout childhood. I wonder, was there a part of me that knew I was being protected? Was some of my bravado linked to my angelic experiences? Did I somehow know that they would watch over me?

The truth is, Angels are always there with us; looking over, waiting for an opportunity to assist, help, and when necessary, protect us. Angels and Guides know us (our strengths and weaknesses) better than we know ourselves. When they interact with us, it is always for our highest good, growth and potential. We may not be able to see the whole picture at first, but eventually we gain a better understanding of their assistance and the significance of their existence. Their interaction in my high school years wasn't obvious to me, but in college their presence became much more pronounced.

> *"This vastness is not empty or a void or impersonal, but filled with the incandescent nectar of selfless love, tender joy, and gratitude."*

—Prajnaparamita Sutra

The College Trip

The Greek Club organized a three-day ski trip to the Poconos. At that time, the Poconos was lauded for their fun-filled weekends. So my brother, some friends and I were excited to go. The snow was plentiful that year, and the weather proved perfect for skiing. It was just a short trip from Queens, and as soon as we arrived, the adventure started. Some sought the slopes, a few set out to see the vistas from the hiking trails, and the rest went horseback riding. Later in the evening, we all met back at the motel to hang around the fire pit. We ate, we drank, we danced and sang...just having a great time and enjoying being young and carefree.

On the second day of the trip, my friends Gus and Mike asked me to join them on the semi-expert mountain for some skiing. I said yes even though I should have said no, considering I didn't have the experience to take on that challenge. I didn't want to give up before even getting a chance to try. Just getting started was difficult since I had never been on a lift. That was where Gus and Mike left me, and I kept trying until I conquered getting myself into a seat. Heading up the mountain, my immediate concern was not that I wouldn't catch up to them. It was more about what I was going to do once I got up there. 'How do I get off this thing?' I said to myself, suddenly realizing I had a fear of heights! As the lift climbed higher and higher, so did the temperature in my ski suit.

There were a couple of opportunities to jump off, but I was too frightened, so I stayed on trying to get the courage. Watching others do it gave me hope, but then once I realized I might slide down the mountain after landing, I couldn't bear to let go. My do-or-die moment came soon enough when I saw Gus and Mike waving up ahead. With their well-needed guidance, I was encouraged to jump. At that point, they caught on that I had no skills and could barely hold myself up on the skis. They asked how long I had been skiing. "Including today?" I said, "One!" They looked at me with concern, and I could tell they were wondering what they were going to do with me next. "Don't worry guys," I told them. "I won't hold you back. Go ahead and enjoy. I'll manage." Mike took advantage of the gesture and started down the mountain, but Gus stayed behind.

Deciding to use the time as a teaching opportunity, he showed me how to slow down, turn, do the side-to-side walk, and most important, how to get myself up after falling. While looking down the mountain, I had an epiphany. How incredibly stupid was I to get on the lift this morning? At that point, it was too late to second guess myself. With Gus right behind me, I started sliding down fast. It was awesome...crazy, but awesome. I momentarily lost my fear and just experienced the fun of it all. As I picked up speed, I saw a cliff and realized I would need to make a turn or take a free fall right off. I thought it best to try a few of Gus' techniques starting with the turn, then stop and fall...in that order. I landed sideways, which broke my speed, but almost got my wrist broken in the process. Gus was impressed since his fall-down-and-stop technique saved me on the first try. He continued to ski behind me for a short while so he could watch a few more of my practice falls, then took off by himself for some real skiing.

After a few minutes on my own, I started to gain confidence, and by the last two turns, I was flying, happy not to fracture a bone. I finished like a pro. Mike found everyone and told them of my escapades, so all were gathered at the bottom waiting for my grand finale. I am not sure whether they were there to cheer me on or watch me land on my rear. When I finally got to the bottom, a few asked how I made it down. I told them, the only way that I knew, "Sideways!" And so that is how I ended my first day on skis.

Angel Hands to the Rescue

The next morning, the guys asked me to join them again. I took a good long gaze at the mountain and wondered how I was able to do it. Looking back I understand how much ethereal help I must have been given. I declined their offer and sat around for the rest of the day watching other people land on their backsides. On the last day of our trip we made plans to rent snow mobiles. I wanted to be first on line, so I arrived early and it paid off. I was the first to get on a sled and receive instructions. While sitting on the cool machine, I couldn't wait to take off and enjoy the ride. I listened, but kept thinking they were taking their job too seriously. How hard can it be? 'Come on already,' I was thinking. 'Let's go!'

Of course, I should have been paying more attention to what the guy was saying, but I didn't, and when he was finished, I took off with a blast. The machine was fast. It was my first time ever on a snowmobile and it was exhilarating, but without knowing what I was doing, I got in trouble just as fast. I ran into a couple of bumps, lost my balance and began to fall off with everyone behind me watching. The actual fall happened rapidly, but in a strange kind of way it felt to me like slow-motion speed.

While on my way down to the snowy ground, I felt two hands grabbing me firmly by the waist. They lifted me up and placed me back onto the seat. I turned and looked behind me to see who it was, but there was no one there. I was looking around full circle, but no one was near enough to me to have helped. Confused and without answers, I sat there on the machine and glanced up toward the sky for possible feedback. 'Who lifted me?' After taking a deep breath, I cautiously continued on with my ride, still feeling the hand grip on my waist. A chill ran through me thinking about what could have happened, but I was still joyful.

Later my brother pulled up next to me and asked what happened. I didn't have a complete answer for him. Can anyone immediately comprehend, let alone explain, a celestial interaction? I don't think so! Do we embrace the reality of a Higher Power at such moments? I believe we can, and it becomes easier when we open our hearts to it. I decided at that time not to speak about the fall. I repressed it until fourteen years later in a meditation class when it came back in a flash. At first, I thought it was my imagination, but then realized it was a real memory. The more I spoke about the fall that day, the more it helped to recover the details. By the end of class, I was left wondering how many other forgotten events I might uncover with meditation. As my odyssey continued, I would discover there were many.

"The intellect has little to do on the road to discovery. There comes a leap in consciousness, call it intuition or what you will, and the solution comes to you, and you don't know how or why."

—ALBERT EINSTEIN

Here I am at eight years old in my class picture, middle row, 4th from left.

A recent photo of the school I attended. Looks more like a prison now.

How things have changed! We couldn't even draw in
pencil on our desks without being scolded.

This is the church my classmates and myself were expelled
from due to our constant outbursts of laughter.

One of my hiding places on the mountain.

A lunch-time location from my days playing hooky on the mountain.

A view from the highest point of my hiding spot.

The sunsets in Greece were beautiful, but very frightening to a little boy on the run!

The place I hurt my eye. The well remains the same to this day.

Part
II

The 'Sun' of God

When I was young, I used to think about how much God and the sun were alike. The sun radiates its energy in order to feed every living thing. Whether it is a piece of fruit, poison ivy, a rose, a toad, or a tree, the sun has no judgment on what it shines its brilliant energy on. It made sense to me then that God shares with us the same way. Whether we are like the rose…someone everyone wants to look at and be around, or we are as unlikeable and untouchable as poison ivy, we can still take advantage of God's goodness.

When we inquire about the sun, we usually ask, "Is it in or out today?" Of course we know the sun is always in the sky, but sometimes when it is raining out we forget that the sun is still shining with all its light and glory behind clouds of gray and black. It is the same with God. No matter whether we are experiencing a joyful, sunny time in our life or a storm full of rain and clouds, God is still there. Often we will turn from the sun because it is too strong for our eyes. Don't most of us also turn away from God at one time or another as well? When we bask in God's light, our uniqueness is exposed, and so too are our issues and perceived flaws. What we need to change, grow and evolve out of becomes highlighted in contrast to the goodness of that divine light. It is difficult to face that much exposure!

Marianne Williamson, in her book, "A Return to Love," says, "*It takes courage...to endure the sharp pains of self-discovery, rather than choose to take the dull pain of unconsciousness that would last the rest of our lives.*" She is insinuating that many of us want to stay numb in favor of being overexposed and vulnerable. That bringing God into our life every day meant we were purposely exposing ourselves to the 'burning' away of our tough, human masks so we can reveal a new version of ourselves, or better stated, to reveal our authentic self. If the sun can make our complexion raw, then can being in the presence of our God make us feel raw as well? How much healing time would we need to do that? How much pain would we be in while our new skin began to rejuvenate? What would our new skin look and feel like afterward? For most, not knowing the answers to all these questions would create much anxiety and of course it would prevent many from exposing themselves to this kind of pain. After all, who would want to put themselves through so much without knowing in the end how things will turn out? But for those of us with the understanding that the most intense growth and awareness cannot come without an intense peeling away, we run towards the heat, even though at any given time, we may have run from it as well.

If you asked yourself how you felt at this very moment, what would you say? "I am joyful," or "I am sad?" "I am guilty and shamed," or "I am strong and convicted in God's Love?" "I am scared and lonely," or "I am fearless and filled with God's power?" Do these questions move you to seek out more light or does it make you want to shut yourself in and close the shades? The ethereal part of ourselves has a constant connection to the frequency of God, but because we are here in a human body having a human experience, our ego (the merely human mind and denser part of ourselves) can dictate our state of being, which, unfortunately can stunt the evolution of our soul and our life. Most of our time and effort during any given day is poured into working, whether it be at home and for our family or for the sake of making money. The rest of our time is spent sleeping, eating, searching, shopping...complaining. All of this translates into an awful lot of time spent on just surviving and or trying to take care of our physical, emotional and mental needs. With all this going on, when do we find time for our soul's needs? God is everywhere in our every day, no matter what we are doing. But are we engaging with God fully?

As the sun exists and is in place whether the Earth is facing it or not, so is God's love still facing us and radiating upon us. God waits for us to expose ourselves. Physically speaking, our bodies don't have to do anything. We exist and are alive because of both God and the sun. Mentally we can perceive God's existence the same as we can see the sun on a sunny day. Emotionally we can utilize the love the same as our neurotransmitters utilize the daylight. All of this happens for us unconsciously, but we can't take full advantage of this guidance unless we spiritually ask for it. No different from going outside to soak in the sun, we need to step into our life with purpose and with God in our focus on all planes of existence. It is important to note, too, that being aware of and wanting to receive more of God's love doesn't make more love come in. The love is and was already there! Asking of ourselves to absorb God's goodness and to reflect that goodness in all we say and do is what we have to remember to do! When the sun rises to a New Day, so can we. Our desire to be in light is always a decision away.

If you are curious at any given time to know how much of God's light you are allowing to shine upon you and through you, it can be partially measured. Look at the way you are moving through life. Are you perceiving it as joyous, loving and carefree? Or are you a victim waiting for life to unfold before you? Are you acting with love and goodness in your heart? Or are you angry and unforgiving? Think about whether or not you are taking advantage of the light that is being offered by going out every minute and soaking it up (allowing love to come in), or spending time locked in your house (closing your heart) with the shades down unwilling and afraid to see or feel the light that is out there. The more of God's light, love and life we allow in, the more joy and freedom we experience.

Lucky for us, we are acquiring all of this with more than just the decision we make in our mind. There is more to us that is interacting with God than we are consciously aware of. Our souls' spirit is interconnected with Source, and that energy is always within us influencing our direction. It would stand to reason that each of us takes in and consumes as much as we can handle at any given time, because if we were to take all of it in at once, it would demand a total revamp of every human mindset and belief system we have gathered to date. Many of us want to hold onto the limited aspects of ourselves and we tend to block out God's light when we feel uncomfortable. We want to be human, because being anything else requires too much effort and most often, pain. We sometimes just want to do what we can get away with or what comes easy, not what we are being led to do for the sake of goodness and growth. None of this human stuff allows for much light, does it? The truth is, the amount of God's love and light we are each willing to expose ourselves to will vary on what energy and emotions we are willing to manipulate within ourselves. If we wanted God to have true freedom with our lives and heart, we would need to say, "My will is Your will." So what we are essentially putting out there in prayer is, "The sky is the limit, and You know best! I trust You. Go for it!" We have to be ready and able to go in whatever direction God's will takes us. Tall order for any human for sure! Luckily, when we say this prayer, we are automatically taken out of our own way. We don't have to be afraid of moving too fast either. God knows what we can handle, and we are never going anywhere alone. The 'sun of God' always shines within us as well as on us.

Energy as a Life Force

God's love is the energy sustaining every living thing on earth, including 'all there is.' Much exciting and confusing information exists out there that let's us know there is something far greater at work than just what we can see and understand. Even if we were to just speak scientifically...on a molecular level...we can come to the conclusion that there is no separation between us and the universe. Our bodies are made of the same minerals, nutrients and amino acids as everything that exists. We know now that planets influence each other energetically as do we influence each other. We know our bodies function as energy processors; consuming food for energy, burning calories for energy, sweating and excreting to allow for more energy. We are just starting to learn how our bodies become healed and energized by the powers that exist outside of ourselves. Studies show that just being in the powerful energetic pulse of the forest, the ocean or mountains has been proven to right the wrongs in our body. Makes me wonder…if science is leading us to this, then why would we still be led to the drug store to heal a cold instead of being sent into the forest?

Everything is all about energy. We know when our energy is low when we slow down and get tired, feel drained or depleted. Some of that occurs because we depleted the body by not taking care of it properly, but much of it is stress, perception and emotions…ours and other people's. We are all connected and have the potential to feel everything around us that is negative or positive, good or bad, beautiful or ugly. Although I don't always focus on just energy when in the company of others, I can always feel when positive energy is emanating from them. When we feel good in the presence of another, it is because we can feel positive (or similar) energy coming from them. In other words, we resonate with them, their frequency and their aura. I think of the body as the human focal point we can use as a reference to determine where we (or others) are at with the mind and spirit.

Although science is precise and can explain much about energy, there is still so much we don't know. I'm usually confused by it and sometimes put my intellect in when I should just allow for information to enter. Once on a flight bound to Europe, I saw on the TV monitor our plane's altitude, speed, and outside temperature. It read thirty-five thousand feet, six hundred miles per hour, and forty degrees below Fahrenheit, respectively. I was sitting by the window enjoying the warmth of the sun wondering why it got colder outside the cabin as we got higher even though we are getting closer to the heat. I usually put the thoughts aside, but they come back. Ideas, thoughts, and curiosities about the sun always re-ignite, and now that I have more access to information through the internet, I can research answers. That would satisfy most, I guess, but I always find more is better.

"Life is a state of consciousness."

—EMMET FOX (1886–1951), AMERICAN SCIENTIST,
PHILOSOPHER, NEW THOUGHT TEACHER AND WRITER

Staring at the Sun...Not Necessarily a Smart Thing

While attending a metaphysical class about the sun I was able to get in touch with my flaky side. Now when I say flaky, I mean 'out there' with my ideas. For instance, I have persistent questions like, 'Is the sun a spirit? Is it a gateway to another existence? Who can prove what the sun really is?' So I was in my element and thrilled with the ideologies of this new group who believed, and I quote, "Sun is intelligence radiating on the highest frequency. The more you can receive of its radiant loving energy, the closer one gets to God's frequency." Now that's what I'm talking about! That statement alone was worth the trip for me. With this ideology, a how-to was offered, and after the suggested preparation, I was ready to download the sun's high frequency energy. Being my autonomous self though, I undertook the experiment without following the method. In other words, I did my own thing.

Basically and very stupidly, I gazed at the sun long enough to cause permanent damage to my eyes, but I am sure the situation could have been even worse. I remembered my childhood Asian teacher warning me, "When older, you'll be tempted to do some stupid things. Some you'll avoid, others...?" Well, I can't say he was wrong. I can imagine he told my Angels to look out for me. If I were to make a checklist of how many times I have done stupid things and needed the Angels, like when I was chased by the mason, check; while skiing, check; while driving, check; while drowning, check; while going blind gazing at the sun, check! While putting hands on hot charcoals while attending a tepee ceremony (you'll hear about that one later), check; and so much more...check, check, check, and check.

Everyone gets into trouble. And everyone's trouble is special and unique since we each get triggered and sabotage ourselves in different ways. Not-fully-thought-out episodes are my downfall. After my gazing-at-the-sun ordeal, I met a few people and in light (pun intended) of what they shared, I am not the only sun gazer. Fortunately, they didn't get permanent damage during their gazing experiences.

Considering we are human, we all need an ego check from time to time. The permanent burn spot on my eye is mine. Truthfully, we don't need to gaze at the sun to know that life here on earth wouldn't exist without its life-sustaining and loving light. The warmth coming from the sun's rays is not just temperature warmth for the physical body; it has a soulful warmth. It is happy, up-lifting and a gentle touch that generates a soothing inner heat that can invigorate our heart and soul. It is the ultimate and absolutely necessary energy that nourishes all living things. I consider it our super booster, and it offers never-ending love and nurturing fuel for life. In our physical reality in this body and at this time on Earth, it may very well be what is allowing God's pulse to radiate through us. No wonder it feels so good to be in it. Thank you, Sun, for all of your love and your light. I humbly thank you for not blinding me, and also for all of the cancer-free tans throughout the years.

"When there is a moment that you can't find love in your heart, start searching for it with a smile."

—KIROS

Sedona

A beautiful, expansive blue sky caressing red mountains all aglow with golden sun crystals are more than enough to cause me to look into the sun's gaze once again. "Hey you, want to go blind?" said my friend Evelyn, interrupting my gaze, and thankfully too since I would have stayed lost a while longer. "Oh yeah, thanks," I remarked. "What a beautiful place!" I meant it wholeheartedly. Arizona was incredible. My friend, originally from New York, had recently moved, and I was there to visit. We met in a meditation class just months before and quickly bonded having many of the same interests and curiosities about healing and metaphysics. We both had a different approach to spirituality than most of the people I knew, and I enjoyed her perspective and openness. She was a leader though, not a follower like me...a habit I know I needed to break out of. Evelyn's good judgment came in handy on many occasions. In fact, I wish I knew her sooner! I relished in the grace, inner wisdom, and confidence she exuded. She would call me 'the sponge' because of the endless list of questions I would ask. In a short period of time, we both grew a fondness and mutual respect for one another.

When she offered me a place to stay if I were ever to visit Sedona, I jumped at the chance. The trip was about a year after I took Reiki training and had packed in many meditation, yoga, and intuitive courses. I thought that my psychic abilities, intuition, healing, awareness, and perception were open and growing, but wanted even more expansion. Since Sedona was considered a vortex and 'hot spot' in the metaphysical world, I was eager to take some workshops and lectures. Turns out that Sedona was to a psychic sponge the same as Disney World is to a child.

Evelyn had a tough time containing this sponge's enthusiasm. I was like, "Eeny, meeny, miney, moe, pick a master for your growth!"

The natural beauty of the area makes for an even more spiritual ambiance. There were majestic mountains everywhere, reminding me of my years in Greece. I took drives to each, hopping from one to the other, chasing the energy and having fun exploring the terrain. I never felt so welcomed, and it wasn't just the people that made me feel at home. It was all of it. I felt love from the ground, the sky and the air. Sounds too crazy to be real, but it was so real to me. With Evelyn's helpful directions, I was able to visit plenty of energy hot spots, attend a few dynamic workshops and lectures, and then spent many hours with other psychics, healers, energy workers, and intuitives. All of it noticeably uplifted my awareness.

And Cindy Makes the Power of Three

A few days into my visit, Evelyn's friend Cindy joined us on a day trip to the Red Rocks at Sedona. Cindy was a Reiki master and intuitive so we made quite a flaky threesome. I drove first, which may not have been the best idea since I was trying to take in the scenery and navigate at the same time. After a couple of mishaps, Evelyn took the wheel. Now having the luxury of being a passenger, I was able to fully enjoy the scenic and very heavenly views. The conversation was refreshing as well, and the three of us were jabbering and completely in sync with each other the entire trip. On one road turn, instead of remarking with 'oohs' and 'ahhs' about the beautiful scenery we saw, we all said sadly, "Oh, what happened?" It wasn't that the view wasn't beautiful; it was. We saw red, clay-colored ground with bright green pine trees and red rocks strewn all around. It was just plain awesome, but it felt unhappy.

While driving through all three of us started remarking about our sensations. Cindy felt thirst. Evelyn felt like crying. I had a sense of anger. Not knowing what to make of it, Evelyn suggested we turn around and pull over. As she made the u-turn, Cindy asked to leave. I wasn't sure which way to go. "What's going on here?" I said. "It looks great, but it feels heartbreaking, like there is a sense of pain, despair, and confusion in the air. Definitely this place can use a healing." They concurred. "What kind of a healing?" I asked. Evelyn suggested we all focus to see what came up, and Cindy and I agreed.

Rain Makers

We got out of the car, found a place to sit and started tuning in. Evelyn was the first to stop meditating, then Cindy. Both sat quietly and waited for me to finish. "OK, guys, I'm done." I said, "What did you get?" Cindy said, "I feel the trees are not happy for some reason; not sure why though; they look so beautiful." Evelyn chimed in, "I feel that the ground is very dry and angry. I think it is because it hasn't rained for so long." They both waited for me and then asked laughing, "What did you get?" "I saw images," I said. "It was of the elements of air, water, and of the earth, and I'm sensing that for some reason they have no connection. I don't understand what that means, but my intuition tells me that we need to help them connect." They looked at me curiously and simultaneously asked, "But how?" Now I was laughing. "I don't know! Let's pray for them to find peace and ask for rain to happen for the benefit of all." "Sounds good to me," Evelyn said. "It hasn't rained much for a year from what I hear. And there is a big problem with water this year. The reservoirs are down to 10 percent, and there is a major problem with neighboring states and water rights. Arizona has been desperate to resolve the issue." We agreed to pray together, asking for guidance so we could be of service to all for the highest good. We ended with a resounding, "Amen!" We stood in a circle and held hands, thanked God for the opportunity to be of service and for the angels assistance in hearing and answering these prayers. We hugged each other, got into the car, and headed off to our destination.

The next day, it rained, and the day after that, and the day after that. My visit finally ended, but Evelyn let me know that in the weeks to come, enough rain fell upon the state to fill the reservoirs to capacity. That is the stuff memories are made of, but there was so much to cherish about Arizona from the royal blue sky and endless stars at night to the glorious sun and majestic mountains, most especially, the wonderful people. I will never forget the amazing energy Sedona offered. Since that trip, Cindy moved to Germany and Evelyn passed away, but before they both left, we were able to speak about the healing the three of us facilitated on the side of the road.

It is my belief that Evelyn had a tremendous gift and was able to communicate with the elements. Cindy and I, both well meaning, gave our best effort and were probably the impetus that brought Evelyn there to do her work. She was humble and never shared much about the work she did while traveling all over the world. She was an earth angel for sure! God bless.

Testing the Waters

Since then I've met others with similar gifts who could connect with the elemental forces and change the weather. These changes were documented, and I don't believe they were coincidences. I truly believe some people have these types of abilities. Not all shamans do though. A story comes to mind of me and about 15 other brave souls rushing to gather wood for a huge fire we had started. It was being used to heat up special rocks for a sweat lodge ceremony, and rain clouds were gathering. The shaman we were with requested our help to find wood to place around the fire. Without using a filter on my mouth, I blurted out, "Why don't we just stop the rain?" He gazed at me with slanted eyes as he picked up a piece of wood, and I'm sure he considered hitting me over the head with it.

Truthfully, I didn't mean to be disrespectful, just adventurous. I was expecting more of a perky smile and a 'Let's do it bro!' than a bitter glance. With the friends I was surrounding myself with at that point, I would have gotten a hardy laugh or even a few to take on the challenge, but not this guy. The shaman did get a chance to get back at me later on at the sweat lodge ceremony. While I was trying to cope with the intense heat (think lobster bake), a sizzling amber from the fire flew up and landed on my shoulder. My eyes were closed though, and thinking that the burning sensation was part of my body's response to the detox, I stayed in my pose and didn't think to look at what was sizzling on my skin. How crazy to be so dedicated to the process that I didn't use my common sense to open my eyes and look to see what was burning. I'm certain the shaman saw the hot amber and enjoyed every minute of my apparent stupidity.

And that wasn't the only "stupid" assumption I had. While in there, I kept seeing people suddenly bow and thought at first it was because they were trying to be one with the earth out of respect. Then I realized it was because steam travels upwards and the lower you are the cooler it is! Few of us were able to sit up straight since the steam was so intense, but the more experienced attendees knew enough to timely bow when the steam rose. Live and learn, then learn some more.

"To love yourself is to love and thank all of existence."

—MASARU EMOTO

The Odyssey of a Healer Starts with a Question

I always wanted to know the reason why we as humans have physical discomforts beyond our body's ordinary friction. Is an emotion that is attached to a health concern fueling that health concern, or is it the other way around? And as healing goes, what is the priority of focus in the attempt to help people; is it to heal their emotions, their physical symptoms, or both? There is also an obscure relationship between a chronic health issue and the drama or emotion that accommodates and supports it. As the years progressed and my proclivity towards the healing arts became evident, these were the questions that fueled my desire to keep learning. But before getting to awareness about health, dis-ease and healing, there was a need to further my understanding of what it means to have a healthy body, mind, and spirit. To have deep awareness, most of us need to go on a journey of self discovery to fully appreciate the gift of life we have been given. Some need to suffer from illness, recovery, or acceptance of disease. All of this will inevitably lead to more gratitude for health in general. What if illness or tragedy doesn't befall us though? How do we come to this deep appreciation without trauma?

Perhaps having an innate understanding of the importance of the mind/body/soul connection acts as the prelude to a healer's odyssey. I somehow had the sensitivity and deep awareness of the gift of life without needing to go through a tragic illness. It was my destiny to become a healer. The constant questions may have fueled my need for knowledge, but the gifts were present before I understood how to use them. It is important for any gifted practitioner to understand the process of self growth. The more we heal ourselves, the more gift we will be utilizing to heal others. In other words, I needed to clear away all facets of humanness and ego that would get in the way of my healing techniques. The first question any of us should ask before embarking on this odyssey: "How motivated am I to become the best I can possibly be?"

Healing Energies Warrant a Healer's Attention

While I was immersed in my learning process, it made sense that more people were drawn to me to heal them. This really triggered my need to become more focused and concerned about the methods I was using. While attending healing circles, other healers were experiencing similar results. We uncovered the commonalities, and when we gathered our findings, we were able to decipher fact from coincidence. It forced me to look closely and deeply with a whole new perspective of my client's behavior, expressions and reactions. I used this to study the cause and effect of their symptoms.

Some of the Reiki circle attendees were what I called 'repeaters.' Their symptoms were always the same and ranging from stiffness, pains, and aches, to whatever else was causing resistance. At the time, it puzzled me. Often after treatment these people felt great, but by the following week, they would come back with the same symptoms all over again. Some people would experience spontaneous healing and not return, but the ones that came back warranted more research. I asked the teacher and wasn't happy about the answers I received. "People heal at their own pace," was one such answer. "They don't let go," was another. The list was long, including surrendering and lack of self love. I can look back now and conclude that all is true, but then why bother coming to a healing circle in the first place? There was a dichotomy going on within each person who was not being healed. There was a side to them that was concealed and was preventing each from getting well, feeling better and healing. I wanted to know what it was and how I could get to it.

I started to pay more attention to people's inward and outward expressions hoping to expose the hidden element. Everyone seemed to react in a sequence, and I wondered if it was all connected. Their recovery and reappearance of symptoms couldn't be labeled, but still I wanted to call it something. Expression of the ego, the subconscious mind, a form of emotional release, resistance to change, trauma, karma...I had many terms. If I wanted to help them release their issue and break the pattern or cycle, I had to know its origin. I had to be able to define it.

There was another element too. I had come to find that some people were not looking to change. They just wanted to be pampered. That made it harder to recognize why they were seeking out help. Was the hidden part keeping them stuck, or was it guiding them to change? Were they coming out of habit? Was this the end result of a repeated cycle of emotional issues? Perhaps, there's an on-going struggle to change within? Maybe some type of physical, mental, or spiritual deficiency? And then there is resistance, but what type of resistance? Is the source of resistance mental, physical, emotional, spiritual, a combination of any and all? I was told consistently not to be attached to the work and for good reason! The more I asked, the more attached to the outcome I became. Essentially I was driving myself crazy.

As I got more involved, I became more confused. It was all part of my journey, but it also filled gaps in what I could now call an empty life. And part of it was my need to satisfy ego. I wanted to stand out and to be different. There was also an inner calling at work that drew me towards becoming a better healer. Another key factor is that I wanted to heal myself. I recognize now how I contributed to a fair share of limitation, conditioning, aches, and discomforts...my own and others I worked with. We are all human and susceptible to our needs, wants, resistance, and doubts. After working consistently on my own intention to heal, I was led to listen more to people's issues and situations. I observed their body language and how they verbalized their pain. I paid attention to my own reactions and took mental notes of everything I was witnessing. All of this helped me connect the dots between emotional expression and physical conditions. I came to recognize unique patterns in each person I worked with, as well as similarities in their emotional behavior and their results. The need to explore these facets was instinctual, and these instincts took me further than what was necessary to be efficient at Reiki. I was in constant need to learn more, and later, I would come to find out why.

Recognizing the Power of Reiki

Reiki has the ability to assist everyone, and there is no need to be versed in the science in order to be effective at it. Its benefits can be partially measured too with before-and-after assessments at the time of treatment. We hope to see obvious change in a client's condition, whether it be physical, mental, emotional, or spiritual. We can't always see or detect it right way though. Irrespective of that, Reiki has the ability to transform one's life and energy in distinct and subtle ways. There are countless miracles to report and testimony to hear that speak loud and clear about its positive effect. This book only includes a short intro and can't compare to the countless resources available. My hope is that this little 'taste' will prompt my readers to seek out other resources and a Reiki master since there are so many expressions of health, wellness, energy imbalances and sickness to explore. If Reiki taught me anything it was that no matter how profound or valuable a treatment is, there is no guarantee another person will have the same outcome.

Besides my own opinion and thoughts about physical discomforts and how they relate to emotion, there are many healers that suggest the cause of all physical/emotional conditions is energy. Whether it is a lack of energy (chi), a block, or a surge, manipulating it can lead to healing. For instance, if we have an injured knee we would investigate what is flowing or not flowing from it. Even if the original cause of the pain was a sustained injury, it all still goes back to how energy is flowing. When a person is healthy, recovery should take place in a reasonable timeframe with only minor assistance. Without a healthy body it is hard to determine.

That brings to mind what we consider healthy. Does it mean a person looks good visually? Have they recently had a physical exam to show that everything is in order? Do they eat reasonably well? Have no pain? Exercise and take supplements? Let's say that a person like a professional athlete, someone who looks amazingly healthy and takes care of his/her body, unexpectedly dies. A stunning example, but it happens, and when it does, we all look at it from a physical perspective. The body is in excellent condition, no doubt, except it has failed to sustain life. It lends itself to more explanation about the whole human expression, and it should lead us to search for more answers about how our bodies express mental thoughts and emotions such as fear of failure for instance. General awareness leads to personal growth, which will lead us to healing, wellness, discovery of our life purpose, self-appreciation, and gratitude for what exists.

I personally wanted to learn as much as I could about healing because I didn't find the traditional approaches effective. In fact, sometimes they were harmful and created other symptoms and side effects. There may be danger incurred when supplementing our energy with another type of energy treatment if we don't know what type we need. Also, we need to know what our practitioner's intentions are, considering they are human and on their own journey. Fortunately, there are some consistent truths we can rely on. First, we are always led in one way or another to the healing modality that is necessary for our growth at that time. And second, we won't ever completely move forward in personal growth until we break away from our current resonating frequencies.

Assuming our practitioner has good intentions and is well versed and trained in the modality we need, what could be wrong with laying on a massage table and allowing a master to work their healing 'magic' on us? The new energy flow is rejuvenating, uplifting, and relaxing and can take us to a soothing and seemingly heavenly place. It's awesome, but it also presents another issue. Afterwards, when the newly facilitated source of energy flow has ended and one's flow starts to take over, what happens then? Is it possible to hold onto that? Unless our own unhealthy patterns are broken, our unique bundle of issues start to resonate deep within. With any energy healing, the hope is that permanent changes can occur, but this can only happen when an intention for such is created, the practitioner and the client is in agreement, and the process resonates with both's belief systems. Lots of concurrent factors need to be present, and it is when all of this comes together that true healing is reached!

> *"Remember that your perception of the world is a reflection of your state of consciousness. You are not separate from it, and there is no objective world out there. Every moment, your consciousness creates the world that you inhabit."*
>
> —ECKHART TOLLE

Is It Karma or Just Plain Ambition?

My desire to learn kept leading to more instruction on healing. Some were practical. Some were not, but if I were to look at it from a karma or law of attraction perspective, everything had its purpose. My ambition took me from learning about energy and how it affects the body, to learning how to actually shift energy and use it to heal. I am happy to admit that when I look back, some of my ego-driven decisions had value. We really do learn from our mistakes once we shift out of the drama they cause! It all breaks down to knowledge that leads to awareness. This combination gives us the necessary means to liberate ourselves from false and preconceived concepts. Some of my knowledge about performance came from observing and comparing the work of other practitioners. What I realized with each new method is that my expectations were high. Each performance was never as good as I wanted it to be. That prompted my need to keep searching for more answers. When I couldn't find them, I felt ineffective. All of this translated into a desperate need to be a better healer, and that desperation actually distracted me from the truth. What I really needed was time to resolve my own limitations, because the 'answers' were always there! They existed within, but instead of relying on what I could glean from my own knowingness, I was constantly searching outside of myself and believed there existed a more valid knowledge base elsewhere.

When the right teachers and opportunities to learn arose, I took them, but instead of accepting them at face value, I made things harder on myself by rating each modality on whether a person healed or not. Not everyone will heal from just one treatment, most especially if they are holding onto ego issues. In any event, I continued to listen to the struggles and triumphs of other practitioners. I sought out teachers, which blinded me from seeing my own reality and kept me from pursuing a journey of self-acknowledgment. Bottom line, I believe I had some obscure notion that everyone else knew what I didn't know. This attitude limited my potential, though there was a lot of excitement and interesting aspects that came with the process, such as; psychic readings, channeling, energy protection, astral projection, mediumship, psychometry, and various energy manipulation techniques such as zapping (projection of energy).

Learning the Not-So-Easy Way

Everyone in my circle used to get zapped back in the day. Not sure why, but there was always lots of chatter about it. The first time I zapped someone it was to see if I could do it, and then I did it again to reinforce that I actually zapped them in the first place. It wasn't smart, but it also wasn't malicious. I was just joining in with some jokesters I had met at a workshop. Thinking back, I shouldn't have modeled my behavior after them, especially when they haphazardly used tools like energy projection. I learned the hard way, unfortunately, but the workshop was about moving and creating energy, so it seemed innocent enough. It wasn't the first time I'd been with this group or was exposed to the work, and I had a certain degree of comfort with everyone. During the lunch break, a few participants were having fun and causing a commotion. Curious, I asked them what was going on. "Check this out!" one of them answers. It was Bob, a thirty-five-year metaphysical veteran with many talents, but unfortunately, little integrity. Since the workshop topic was about his specific expertise, he couldn't resist showing off his skills. He got everyone's attention and started zapping Janet across the lobby about forty feet away. He picked her because her body would involuntarily move and shake while in the presence of intense energy. And did she shake! I don't know how she managed to keep her stability.

The 'monkey' in me wanted some of the attention this other monkey was getting, and so I decided to zap her too. She had no clue what was going on across the room. She was used to being affected by energy though. It was part of her life. She could easily be shaken while on a bus or subway...just about anywhere. When her body encountered energy, it would wobble. For a while, she didn't realize that it was us projecting energy onto her, until the person she was speaking with caught sight of us making gestures at her, and the monkey party quickly came to an end. Janet looked over pointing her finger and shaking her head in disbelief. Feeling remorseful, I went over to give her a hug and apology. She accepted and interestingly enough, she asked me to zap her again later, stating my energy felt good. Not that the behavior should have been condoned, but at least there was no bad karma attached!

Life and It's Lessons Revealed

Whenever a new methodology about healing was presented to me, I wanted to learn everything about it. If it didn't require a lot of time and money on my part, great, but if I thought I was going to learn something important, I would have travelled to the Arctic to get the lesson, which, in fact, I did! Some selections and course studies were probably fulfilling the needs of my ego, but at the end of the roller coaster ride of learning and exploring, I was driven to find out how much of my authentic self could be salvaged. All of it brought me full circle to my childhood. If I had tapped into those early years sooner, I would have saved myself a lot of time and nonsense. Unfortunately, when I got separated from my

Angels, I lost the key to all growth, which is our connection to Source. When we are not connected, the emptiness inside leads us to a life full of sirens, deception, illusions, and more separation.

Life doesn't have to be so hard. The human experience is about letting go, healing, doing better, learning, creating, loving, evolving spiritually, expanding, releasing karma, and of course...the most important...living the life we have been granted by God. And so be it! My thoughts are, let's quickly learn and do it as effortlessly as possible. We should be moving forward and not lost in a spiral wasting precious years. Metaphorically, this is like mimicking Ulysses and others like him. Everywhere we look we can see people (and often ourselves) perpetually stuck in the same conditions, drama, pain, limitations, and illusions.

Fortunately, we don't have to be consciously walking a spiritual path in order to have the common sense to do right for ourselves and everyone else around us. Every person with a conscience can illustrate this. People get driven by their own monkeys, whether it is greed, lust, envy, anger, destiny, drama, suffering, healing, ambition, and others. They become distracted by their needs and desires and also by how they are going to go about getting them. Life teaches us though that what goes around comes around. *"Resist not evil, but whosoever shall smite thee on thy right cheek, turn to him the other also. And if any man will sue thee at the law, and take away thy coat, let him have thy cloak also. Love your enemies, bless them that curse you, do good to them that hate you, and pray for them which despitefully use you, and persecute you."* And can we say the same about Peter after he sliced off the soldier's ear. *"Then said Jesus unto him, put up again thy sword into his place, for all they that take the sword shall perish with the sword."*

There is no teaching of victim-hood or martyrdom here. Why would God create humans in deficiency? I know God did not. Supposedly, it's Adam and Eve's fault, so let us forget our daily trespasses and be in denial until a Divine Being comes and saves us again. They claim there is no need to worry about anything, because it's all going to be taken care of when Jesus comes. With no disrespect intended, that is traditional religious belief that may be leading people to a limited human life without self empowerment or so much as a sliver of opportunity for individual expression or self awareness. If we are waiting for salvation, what are we doing in the meantime?

We have to reach toward God and live within God's presence. Unresolved karma is most likely what is keeping us away from God and from seeing this truth. Until we do, we are being driven (mostly unconsciously) by forces that manipulate our emotional, mental and physical states. Whether we have an understanding of this or not, eventually everyone will align to the process of human evolution. Our souls will not forget the original plan and in time will guide us through the threshold. With mind discipline, focus, diligence, and the gradual advancement of spirit, we can do our best as humans to rid ourselves of whatever is precluding us from seeing truth.

Karma Defined

Karma is a history of energy exchange that is existing within a person that could influence his or her life. There is no doubt in my mind that from birth all the way through to death, karma will play a significant role in directing us. I believe that we come here to live this life and surround ourselves with the people we need to interact with for the sake of healing from shared karma. If this is true, then consider all our early interactions with these people to be the impetus for all our emotional and spiritual work. Suffice it to say, we need to learn from and then clear these connections. It helps to know that people are usually drawn into the energetic connection of karma, and drama ensues as the karma reveals itself. I also think if there is mutual interaction and both sides are feeding the drama, more karma could be created going forward. It stands to reason that if we can identify it as karma sooner rather than later, a healing process will advance faster.

When the factor of karma is considered, it immediately simplifies our understanding of our life experiences and the lessons we are being shown. It also automatically advances us. So recognition is first. Clearing it will then move us forward and through our blocks faster. When we experience overwhelming emotional charges and see lessons repeated over and over, it helps to understand how karmic debt is related. It is like having a life map that keeps showing us the direction we need to take, and it acts like a mirror that reflects back to us, highlighting how we are expressing past events and the connections we have to others. If we were to look into this mirror and make an outline of what we see, karma could then steer our direction towards healing. Finally, karma can help us perceive our whereabouts at any given time and what we are headed toward. It can pull us to what we need to have cleared! All of this can guide us to enlightenment.

Through hypnosis, I have cleared karmic relations in clients, and I find afterward that the release of karmic ties left the client feeling empowered and at total peace. This is what makes regression therapy such an important tool for spiritual advancement. At the same time, through Reiki and other energy modalities, we can heal energetic memory patterns that are attached to emotional and mental abuse, traumas, feelings of anger, despair, confusion, and others. I imagine karmic debt could be paid off regardless if one knows of a technique such as Reiki or hypnosis. If anyone feels a certain obligation to a person or believes there is some kind of hold between themselves and another, it may not be just a typical relationship issue. It could be karma. And when do we know it is karma or just relationship issues? As you can imagine, it isn't easy initially to see the difference.

Part of a healthy state of mind is to have boundaries, and it is good to be able to orally express ourselves to one another, but there is usually more to any story than what is being expressed in the here and now. Sometimes, even when the right sentiment is being expressed by one person, the other one feels an imbalance and tries to gain back their control. Through conflict and struggle we try to manage the emotions and energies, but with only temporary results. The back and forth energetic connection (our writer, D, calls this "The Energy Dance") will continue to cause back and forth drama. Most often we experience this with family members, spouses, lovers, friends and co-workers...people that we share a strong human connection with. And this makes sense from a karmic perspective considering that we need to be in it to eventually resolve it! When it is not resolved, we continue to position ourselves over and over again with blood relations (family karma) or love relations (karmic partners). I consider the concept of karma to be a clever plan used to perpetuate human growth. When in spirit, perhaps we choose our 'payment plan' for any and all debt we collected over lifetimes. And that makes sense, because if we chose the plan while here in human form, most likely fear, anxiety and anger wouldn't let us get too far!

If we were to imagine a karmic relationship as no different from a debt collection, then we would realize how essential it is to relieve ourselves of this debt. If we have a person in our face, relentlessly trying to control us due to our karmic ties, it will leave us feeling powerless. The karma can express itself through poisonous words we will hear echoing in our ears, mind, and heart over and over again. This can negatively affect a normally healthy person's well-being and even more so with someone already ailing or at risk. These actions and reactions cause undo stress that can't be explained in human terms or eradicated with normal stress relievers. It can take away any hope of peace we can find in a day, a week or even years. Fortunately, through spiritual means and positive intention, we can relieve this pressure and resolve our karma. We have to understand that clearing karma, as emotionally intense as it can feel, is the most beneficial energetic hygiene procedure we can undertake for spiritual advancement and physical and mental clarity. Not everyone believes in it or can handle it. The intention to move forward is necessary though in order to start the process, and it is my hope that by the end of this book, you, my reader, will understand karma better and perhaps set that intention going forward.

The Pay Off

Some people ask me if they will know when karmic debt has been paid and if they can feel it. My answer is that it all depends. If we were to reach full enlightenment, suffice it to say, we have probably cleared all karma, otherwise, we wouldn't be that enlightened! It has been my experience that many people play out their karmic debt over and over again and are almost held hostage by their own inability to learn lessons. Luckily, we don't have to know what the karma is in order to pay the debt or release it. We just have to create an intention to do either. I believe everyone gets positioned exactly where they need to be for their spiritual growth, though, regardless of whether they intend to seek it or not.

There is no research to show how purposeful karma release presents itself in everyday life, but with a trained eye and ear, it isn't hard to see patterns in families. I have heard many stories and testimonies from those who have done the work and feel the release of negative emotions like resentment, hatred, anger, anxiety, fear, obligation, guilt...the list is endless. I have also found that the more amplified the drama is, the higher the extent of the debt. After release, family members will relate better, so we would have to conclude that a debt has been lessened or eradicated. The release of negative energy allows for a positive segue into a more harmonious existence. When the intensity of karma lessens, so does the need to be angry or hateful, and when that happens, love, forgiveness and understanding comes more naturally.

What I see too, is that people who are paying their karmic debt, whether consciously or unconsciously, will generate a more positive energy. While we are in the process of unraveling karma, we are understanding ourselves better, and we tend to take the blame off of others. All of this helps us express emotions and thoughts in a more positive manner. When we intentionally seek out the separation of our true essence from the roles we have adopted, we begin to see the truth of who we really are and what we are supposed to be doing here. Though without professional help, it could take any one of us a very long time to determine every single aspect and every single road we need to take on this journey.

Soulfully Speaking...

We all have something in common; namely, a soul, and we can tap into it through our subconscious mind or through regression. We also have an energetic system of information called the aura, where all experiences, good and bad, display themselves. It is like a life recording of events and exchanges. We interact as humans in a physical sense and on an emotional level, but soulfully speaking, we interact through energy attachments and karma. This interaction will occur in subtle ways through psychic energy, astral and ethereal cords. Often we will be given a chance to pay a debt through a temporary relationship. A person will enter our life for just this purpose, and we can call it a 'karmic partnership.' However, if we don't learn and grow from that one relationship, karma may accumulate more unresolved feelings, drama, and such. There is always the potential to carry these unresolved issues with us into the next relationship. So the faces may change, but the energy, the circumstances and the exchanges of behavior can all feel the same. Sometimes it will become more tolerable going forward, because some issues within ourselves have resolved, but the lesson could repeat itself again in the same way.

Any energy we are stuck in will attract the same. The law of attraction applies here. A new circumstance will create another opportunity to look within once again, and this time it may prompt a deeper understanding of the cause and source of the lesson. If only this root digging can be done at the onset! How much time and drama would be saved? I can only imagine, but then again, that wouldn't be life as we know it, would it? Having many chances to resolve karma in a lifetime would lead us to understanding the importance of our actions in the present and the consequences those actions create in our future. Karmic debt is measured by cause and effect. It is the energy of exchange we create based on how we conducted ourselves. Many people believe it is good or bad, but actually, the way we feel about it makes it good or bad. It can be created from an exchange of two people or groups of people. Eventually, it plays out in our lives individually, but we will also observe the entire human race in their evolution on the planet earth. By this statement I am not referring to the 'end of the world' scenario we were told would happen in 2012. I'm speaking more to the Greek saying: *"Not taking care of one's own dwelling, the rumble of its ruins will fall upon them."*

"To go from mortal to Buddha, you have to put an end to karma, nurture your awareness, and accept what life brings."

—BODHIDHARMA

What is Good for the Body is Good for the Soul

And there is another kind of karma many don't think about, that is to say; the debt we will owe to animals. We may think we are putting a dent in this debt by having pets, but I don't believe that will do enough to eradicate the amount of negativity this world is exposing itself to. We hear of the domestic animal cruelty that exists, but what about all the other species? Our whales, dolphins, chickens, cows, hogs, and all the rest that may be crying for help. I think about how we soak our calves in wine so that its meat tastes better. Instead, why not have a glass of wine with dinner and allow the animals to roam like they are supposed to? And crazy thing is, any one of them would happily sacrifice its life to elevate their consciousness and be one with us. We need to act less human and start acting more humane! Just choosing to eat free-range beef, pork, and chicken can help us to create a better life for these animals and at the same time, bring honor to the temple's they are being put into, namely; our bodies. We need to show gratitude and appreciation, and do it with the understanding that these animals have just as important a life cycle as do we.

Is the Grass Greener on the Other Side?

During my travels to Europe, I always find the food to be tastier. Fruits and vegetables are richer in flavor and are more dense, which means they are more nutrient filled compared to the often tasteless and dehydrated supermarket selection we have here in the United States. There is no secret why either. They don't use the same methods to grow or raise them, nor do they use the amount of chemicals, therefore the soil in Europe is not depleted. Thankfully, organic farming is getting more popular in the United States. I support my local growers and believe the cost difference to be inconsequential when I consider how much more I am getting for the money and how much less I am eating because my body is so satisfied.

Understanding food and the role it plays in our bodies and our lives is an excellent way to support and encourage greater health, balance and peace. Physically, mentally and emotionally, we are being manipulated by the chemicals in food. All of it can help us stay in tune spiritually, or it can absolutely make it tougher. We need to be educated consumers for sure, but ultimately, each of us is the only one who knows what's really good for our body's wellbeing. The more we listen to TV and buy into commercial ads, the more trouble we can get into, considering how much manufacturers are putting in the food to make it more addictive, unhealthy and less expensive to manufacture.

The bottom line: Food is not what it used to be, and none of us will be able to stay loving, balanced and peaceful if what we are putting in is toxic, harmful and all about monetary gain. After 'X' amount of years of constant misuse of food, we become another purchasing candidate for the commercial ads, and don't get me started on pharmaceuticals! Are any of these manufacturers and dealers aware of karma? What about the FDA, USDA, or equally responsible biochemists along with other public servants that have allowed this? All in all, we are ultimately responsible for buying it and perpetuating the sale. We are responsible for the shape we find our body in as well.

Our food habits sometimes revolve around emotional more so than physical need. When moods are down, most will crave simple sugars and carbs. When moods are elevated, so are endorphins, making us feel so filled up, we sometimes forget to eat. As our consciousness elevates, we become more mindful and sensitive to our food preferences. We not only want to keep our vessel pure, we become more in tune with the energy of the food we decide to put in our mouth. I often see people become vegetarians, because they have become very sensitive to animals, almost able to feel how they lived and how they were killed. We become more in tune with the chemical makeup of the food as well. Food intolerances and allergies become more apparent. Symptoms are not necessarily heightened, but all of a sudden, we begin to realize where they are stemming from.

Food should not be considered the enemy. It is our fuel and energy source, but what we choose to put in will make the difference between being healthy and being sick; being more aware or more confused; being more peaceful or more uneasy. The better we eat, the better our body (as a processor) will pay us back. Food, in and of itself might not be able to bring us to awareness, but it can help to stunt our ethereal growth for sure! At the very least, we need to buy organic and keep our exposure to unnatural and unhealthy substances as low as possible. And let's not discount our taste buds. Joy and happiness...the bliss we derive from eating the earth's nutritious bounty…can connect us to it, contributing greatly to a 'heaven on earth' experience.

And on the Seventh Day, He Rested…

Even God rested on the seventh day, so don't take for granted the fact that we need rest as well as healthy food. While at sleep and most especially during REM state, I truly believe the ethereal part of us detaches from the boundaries of the physical form and travels to the stars. And even if we become dense and laden down by our own emotional baggage, just five feet of lift could be enough for our ethereal body to rejuvenate. There is no need to worry about how far we travel at night, though, since our spirits understand, and our bodies will respond effortlessly much like it does to breathing. This ethereal body is an intrinsic part of our existence here, and although it can't be measured, it can be captured by what is called 'Aura Photography.' You can also feel it by slowly bringing the palms together without touching. If you try this and can't feel the energy right away, rapidly rub your hands together and then try again. There should be a tingling and buzzing sensation. That is the ethereal you! In order to grow this aspect of ourselves though, we need to know if we are feeding it or starving it. When referring to vibrancy and health, Hippocrates said we must bring about balance to ourselves by having a healthy mind, healthy body, and healthy spirit. There is no order of importance either, as all three accommodate each other and equally contribute to our state of balance. The ethereal aspect needs a restful sleep as much as the physical body and mind. We can't tap into one without the other, and we won't see any enrichment without rejuvenation.

Our bodies can become dense while trying to accommodate a dense reality and existence. When we make an intention to take care of ourselves through exercise, healthy eating, restful sleep and meditation, that intention alone can actually enliven us! Our minds become inspired, our hearts become uplifted, our gut becomes motivated. It is so easy at this point to feel joyfulness and contentment in our lives. It has been said that we can't have a clear mind without a clean body. So true, and without that clear head, how can we take charge of our destiny? Where will a cloudy head steer us to? It is important to state that we don't have to make the choice to be healthy right here and now. We can start at any time, but the longer we take to do it, the longer it takes to reach our full potential. Why wait? I am of the belief that it is our birthright to receive everything in life effortlessly. We make it harder than it has to be. We can allow our 'monkey' to guide us to junk food, or our ethereal self to choose organic vegetables. Moderation can dictate the beginning of your journey to wellness as you learn about what your body can handle and what it can't. For myself, the journey to complete mindfulness about eating habits came gradually as I became a vegetarian, started buying organic and eating gluten free. Obtaining alkalinity was a plus too, since disease and cancers cannot survive in an alkaline state.

Choose Peace Over Chaos

What surrounds us can be stressful, but what is inside of us can remain blissful. We make that decision. And when we decide that the temple we house our ethereal self in deserves to be in balance, we handle all of what is going on in our environment in the most peaceful and profound manner. Because of media, we are inundated every day with more and more to deal with than we really have to be exposed to. For most of us, work is stressful too. It exposes us to many other energies and drama from co-workers, clients, and bosses that we allow to put expectations and demands on us. All of this can re-arrange our peaceful state. It would seem almost impossible to stay healthy and balanced in mind, body, and spirit under such conditions. In my experience, using relaxation CD's can help undo the 'amping up' that our perception brings to our minds and bodies. It is important to remember that it is just perception. Everything that happens to, in and around us can be handled in any number of negative or positive ways. When we take into account the condition of our bodies, minds and emotions, we can see how each can play a role in our current perception. Our emotions can be triggered by what is happening in this moment or one from our past (in this life or others). It can be twisted by our unhealthy body, biochemistry or trauma we have accumulated. It can be our own emotion or maybe it is what we are picking up from the person next to us!

When we are mindful of clearing and cleansing ourselves, our perception will change, and we can become more peaceful. In a more cleansed state, everything is interpreted differently, so nothing is perceived the same! All of our breakthroughs, our awakenings, and our moments of self-realization come when the mud we collect living our earthly existence gets washed away. The more we cleanse, the more we allow our ethereal selves to emerge. If we don't, we will remain hypnotized by a negative state of being, further distracted, and, of course, stuck.

We Have to Start Somewhere

To start any spiritual journey it is easiest to first start with the body. Focusing on becoming our best physical self automatically fortifies our mental state, which prepares us for the upheaval that unblocking our emotions, karma and traumas will cause. When we start any journey into transformation, it immediately changes the energy within ourselves and what we exude to the outside world. In other words, just changing our bodies slightly (as in diet, sleep and exercise) can change our energy and eventually all we attract and give out! It also changes our mental state. Since our mental state dictates our perception of loss and deprivation, in addition to our levels of self esteem, self empowerment, self love, and self confidence, we need our minds to be fortified. The good news is that even if our levels of esteem and confidence are low, we can still believe we are worthy of goodness and healing. This is important to understand before we undertake the work. Worthiness is not attached to esteem. If we are willing, we are worthy! And when we perceive all karma and trauma as lessons instead of punishment, we won't feel negative emotions like fear, anger, sadness or despair that the karma might uncover.

Tools for Our Journey

Since the body, the earth and our spirit essence are so complicated, we might not be able to fully grasp all that we possess internally and externally to advance without help on our wellness journey. So we have tools at our disposal. I have attended many New Age expos and have bought my share of stones, crystals and energy boosting gadgets like pyramid-shaped wire to wear on my head. (Are you getting a visual on that one?) Most offer a temporary fix, and depending on the mechanic who created it and the person who is using it, all can offer assistance. Let's take a pendulum for example. It is used to measure and repair chakras. Although there is much controversy over how many we actually have, there are seven main energy centers everyone can agree on. Starting from the bottom of our spine, we have the root chakra, and it represents our foundation and groundedness. The second is called the sacral, and often times considered the sex chakra, it helps us accept new experiences. The third is called the solar plexus because of its location on the body, and it is where confidence stems from. The fourth is the heart chakra and speaks to our ability to love. The fifth is the throat and communication. The sixth is our third eye and how we view the world. Finally, we have the seventh and most important for our spiritual growth, which is the crown chakra. It gives us the ability to connect the ethereal essence that is within, with all that is and exists outside of ourselves. It is what all of this journey is about and is associated with pure bliss.

1- Root **Chakra**: Location is at the base of spine in tailbone area. The emotional issues attached are survival, money and food.

2- Sacral **Chakra**: Located in the lower abdomen about 2 inches below the navel and 2 inches in. Emotional issues include abundance, well-being, pleasure and sexuality.

3- Solar **Plexus Chakra:** Located in the upper abdomen in the stomach area. Emotional issues can include low self worth, self confidence and self esteem.

4- Heart **Chakra**: Located in the center of chest just above heart. A closed heart creates emotional issues surrounding love, joy, inner peace.

5- Throat **Chakra:** Located in the throat. Emotional issues include communication, self expression, truth.

6- Third Eye **Chakra:** Located between the eyebrows. A blockage can make it difficult to hear or connect with our own intuition, imagination and wisdom. It affects our ability to think and make decisions.

7- Crown **Chakra:** Located at the very top of the head. Any emotional issues surrounding it can render us unable to see inner and outer beauty and threaten our connection to spirituality.

When using a pendulum to measure chakra strength, steadily hold the device over one location at a time. Anywhere from a few seconds to a minute, the energy of the chakra will cause the pendulum to move in a certain direction, be it sideways back and forth or around. Depending on what instructional teachings we follow, each range of motion corresponds to a chakra condition and will help indicate if it is opened, closed or blocked; whether it is large or small, etc. When curious about our chakras, these tools can be informative, but we need to keep everything in perspective as they are not always correct. I use them, but rely more on my intuition. I also seek out the help of experts. Until we feel powerful enough to trust our own intuition, we often get help from our Angels in the form of validation from others. This can be a positive experience when we are in the company of the right people.

Whether we are looking for a tool or practitioner, though, we need to be clear about what we need and why. Ask a lot of questions and get a sense of the energy surrounding that person or tool. If it is a service we are seeking, it is less tangible, but we can ask for testimonials and references. If it is a tool, it can be held in our hands, and it will resonate as helpful or it will not.

Reiki as a Tool

If I were to consider everything I have learned to be my tools, my most powerful would be Reiki. It rebooted me after taking a 24 year sabbatical from Angel interaction. I felt this amazing reboot as an uncanny shift in my practice. One day while working on a client, I felt more energized than usual. It was as if I had five expressos and couldn't stay centered and still. Thinking oxygen would help, I took a couple of deep breaths, but it did nothing to calm me down. Thankfully, the woman I was working on was a regular, and I felt comfortable enough to talk to her about it. "Carol," I said, "there is something going on with me today, and I'm not sure what it is, or if I can work with you." I continued exasperated, "I can't stay still!" "Oh," she said, "that's cool. Why don't you relax and let go, and let's see what happens." I didn't expect that answer and wasn't sure where 'letting go' would lead the session, but went ahead with it anyway.

It would help to know that most Reiki practitioners before even touching their clients have already arranged a tranquil room with dim lighting and soft music. We have a client lie face up on a clean massage table with their head resting on a soft pillow and a towel partially covering their eyes. The intent is to have the person be comfortable, relaxed and receptive throughout the entire session. It also helps the practitioner connect to their divine source. At the onset of Carol's session, all systems were go, but for whatever reason, something was out of sync. Starting again to raise my hands over her forehead, I began to tremble out of control. Good thing her eyes were closed, because I looked like a drunken surgeon attempting his first cut. Realizing this, I stopped myself and asked for reassurance. "Carol," I said, "my hands are shaking a lot. Are you sure about this?" With confidence she said, "Keep going and don't worry!" I continued, but kept my hands a little distant. Half way through the session, the trembling became a sort of tapping. I was worried she could feel it, and she did, but said it felt like an energy radiating out from my hands.

When the session was over, I asked her how she felt. "I have to tell you," she exclaimed, "it was amazing! Never have I felt so good. I'm glad we went for it!" She started bending her back and neck, then moving her arms to show me her increased range of motion. "Let's do this again soon!" she said as she gave me a big goodbye hug. As soon as she walked out the door, my questions started. 'What was that all about?' At the time, I didn't have a full understanding of any other innate energy beyond Reiki or my power to do it. I called my Reiki teacher right away, and she assured me it was all okay and not to worry about it. "It will pass," she said. I didn't fully understand what would pass or if I wanted 'it' to! I let the questions in my head dissolve, though, knowing I would see Carol again the following week. I was sure more answers would eventually come.

Knowledge is Power...

Since starting the Reiki practice, I had come to find that certain people were really not interested in healing or soul searching, my friends and family among them. Some were actually uncomfortable just speaking about it, and that translated into my lack of confidence in myself. No blame, but the general lack of trust and faith, not only in me, but in the Reiki process as well, made it harder to realize my potential. This was one more reason I felt the push to learn everything there was to know about healing. The importance of a good teacher and support from like-minded individuals can't be stressed enough. Sometimes, the journey steers itself, and we can become confused. A knowing and well-intended teacher can guide and inform making the trip so much easier. And there is so much to learn in terms of energy healing. As I delved in, I discovered more about myself, and my own abilities emerged. I noticed I was in tune with loved ones. Once in a while I would be asked to work on a family member or friend who may have been doubtful but desperate enough to try anything. When their guard was down, I was able to put more energy into the work. Unfortunately, that sometimes backfired.

An Interesting Way to Catch a Cold

One day I worked on a friend who had a very bad cold that was turning into pneumonia. The medications he was taking were not effective, but that was probably because he wasn't willing to take off from work to allow his body to heal. I worked on him diligently, but by the end of the session I developed all the symptoms of pneumonia as well. It was scary to say the least! I had similar experiences prior to that, but none as intense. He left feeling fine, but I had no idea what to do for myself. It was kind of late in the day, and I didn't feel comfortable calling my teacher to ask for guidance again.

Common sense dictated my own Reiki session and a hands-on-chest energy exchange, but my anxiety and fear got in the way of the flow. If I was a well-trained practitioner at that time, I would have cut off the energetic ties right after the session, and no symptoms would have been transferred. I was still learning, though, and this type of thing was actually what I was in training for. The next morning I ended up calling my teacher, and she laughed. "Oh, you're very empathic!" she blurted out. So that is how I found out that I was an empath. After hanging up though, I wasn't sure if that was a good thing or bad! In my head I kept hearing the words, "Ti epatha," which in Greek means "What has happened to me?" After researching, I learned how to shut down my own aura and to undo the merging of energies with others when this does take place.

Lessons Learned

An empath has the energetic ability or tools to sense how other people experience life and what it feels like to be them. The empath can merge with another's energy consciously or unconsciously, and as they do, they experience mood shifts, physical or emotional pain, and even thoughts. If someone were to spend their lifetime as an empath without understanding the gift or utilizing any skills to offset it, they could live in a state of perpetual emotion. It could seem as if they were living in another's nightmare. Just think of how it would feel to constantly absorb other people's emotional baggage. It helps to know that empaths are born as such. It is a gift with many degrees of strength, and there are several types. Here are a few brief descriptions accompanied by an example of what each specific empath might ask:

Spiritual Empath: Able to feel the presence and energies of spirits or how others connect to God. "I understand a form of religion not familiar to me."

Physical Empath: Able to feel other people's physical symptoms in your own body. "I feel a back ache I didn't have a moment ago."

Emotional Empath: Able to feel another person's emotions. "I am starting to feel nervous for no apparent reason."

Animal Empath: Able to hear, feel and communicate with animals. "I think the dog needs to be walked."

Nature Empath: Able to read, feel and communicate with nature and plants. "I think it's going to rain later today."

Intellectual Empath: Able to assume the intellect and awareness level of another. "I hear and understand exactly what you are trying to say!"

The toughest job of any empath is to separate themselves from what they are perceiving. Although I began to learn how not to merge, I wouldn't perfect the skill until many years later. There were many techniques to try, and some were effective while others, not so much. I learned not to be anxious about merging and for a while, I did well. Every so often I would feel various pains and discomforts, but I was able to alleviate them. Gradually they would catch up with me, and then again, I was challenged to remove them. It was my number one concern through the years, and I would always ask teachers I'd come across the same million dollar question; "How does one go about not picking up other's stuff?" Their answers were all the same: Let it go; burn sage; take baths; ground yourself; dance naked on a rainy day...well I just made that one up!

Drum Roll Please!

Talking about teachers, some years ago I was invited to join some friends at a tepee ceremony. It was to be an all night drumming and chanting session. I was excited to accept since I had never been involved in anything like it before. I loved to drum and had a drum of my own. The ceremony was taking place out on Long Island about an hour away from me in Queens. I only had an address and one directive, "Make a left turn a couple of miles after exiting the highway." The description of where I was heading was something like, 'secluded woods to conceal the smoke, fire and the sounds of beating drums.' The farther out on Long Island I got, the more anxious I became. After two hours of searching and debating a U-turn, I managed to get there. Smoke signals would have been helpful! The only thing that did actually guide me were the many cars I saw parked in the middle of no where.

At first glance it was a mixed group of male and female. In the metaphysical world, there are usually more females attending events, but this was a shamanic, very male-driven ceremony. Nothing else was unusual, and I was happy to see a few familiar faces. Their presence made me feel more comfortable about being there all night. Small talk and preparations ended when everyone started to enter the teepee. From the outside it looked too small to fit everyone, but after getting in there I was surprised to see how much bigger and taller it was. We all found a comfortable sitting spot after 'sensing' where we should be. That is a new-age thing for sure. After stepping in and not seeing all my friends, I actually stepped back out. They were still outside in deep discussion about 20 feet away. "Hey, what's going on?" I said, interrupting their conversation. "Come on, we are about to start." One of the women, Betty, said furiously, "I'm not going in. There's no way!" I couldn't imagine why, so I asked. Elaine then chimed in, "They just told us that we can't be in the ceremony wearing underwear." Amused and confused, I said laughing, "What are you talking about? Stop kidding around. We are going to lose our spots. Let's go!" Elaine said, "There's no joke. The shaman's assistant came and told us there is no underwear allowed in the tepee ceremony!"

Well, thank goodness for Betty, the underwear rebel, because what did I know about teepee tradition or mischievous teachers. All together there were eight of us and six were females, five of which refused to comply. I give a lot of credit to my friend Betty who stood up to the nonsense. We finally took our spots, with the permission of the instructor. Albeit unnecessary nonsense, the foolery didn't keep us from finally joining in. We took turns leading the drumming and also participated in singing. Things got more serious when a horrible powder and drink were offered, followed by a smoking pipe that most of us tried at least once. We weren't told why we should take the medicine, but since it brought us to an altered state, it was most likely supposed to drop our guard. Looking back, perhaps the intention of the night was to bring out any inner negativity and express ourselves in our own unique fashion. One by one our hearts were being affected during the rite, allowing the fire, the drumming, the singing and the heat to all take effect. It was easy to recognize everyone's need for connection to spirit, including my own, but I wasn't sure how much I wanted to let go in order to make this connection. As the night progressed, there was some yelling and lots of crying. It felt a little crazy, and we continually glanced at one another and quietly discussed whether we were getting the full experience.

I will admit that at that time, I didn't have much to compare it to, but still, I was not sold on its validity or the sanctity of the process. As far as I was concerned, a couple of nuances to the evening definitely lacked integrity. The shaman was orally abusive to the group who were his loyal followers and wannabe natives. Male or female alike, he made them cry while breaking their 'spirits' down. Maybe it was a shamanic practice to clear emotional blocks this way, but to me his behavior didn't seem competent and appropriate. I stuck it out, though, and came to find later that not all ceremonies, especially the ones that take place under a teepee, are done in that way. This event proved to me that some spiritual gurus and teachers are not well-intended or experienced. In the future when I asked to join in any group, I would go down a mental checklist to determine whether I should go or not. 'Is the person who is inviting me balanced in their own lives? Do they have energy addiction? Can I recognize growth in them after these experiences? Is their monkey in check?' After objectively analyzing and reasoning, I then feel how it resonates with my body. After all that, I take action. I have saved myself much nonsense by being diligent with my time and money.

Chief Ola

Some of my adventures with teachers were awesome, but gave me something to think about. While on a spiritual quest in Lapland, a province of Finland, I met a shaman chief named Ola. When people happened to get lost in that part of the world, it was Ola who was called upon to rescue them. And I can attest to Ola's survival skills since I went on a quest with him. In a matter of minutes, I watched as he quickly found sticks in the middle of a snowstorm and erected a teepee with them. It was as if he already knew where they were in the midst of all the whiteness. While drying our ourselves in front of a roaring fire inside his amazing structure, we watched his wife prepare elk stew and home-made bread and butter...the best I had ever tasted. Unfortunately, the next day I found out that the elk was only a baby, and its life was taken during a weather ritual. Although I was a vegan for over two years, I ate it out of respect for Ola and his wife, but if I knew it was a ritual, I would have never touched it. I was saddened to hear that people were still using animals in rituals. The idea of shedding animal blood for human gain or empowerment doesn't resonate with me. There is no justification or reasoning that would make sense either. Respectfully speaking, I think an old belief system dictates this behavior. And I also believe that as we align and shift into having more interaction with The Divine, we will also shift out of the notion that we are more important than animals.

Not All Workshops are Built the Same

When I decide to attend a workshop or class, I'll do a 'go see.' If I like what I see and hear, I'll stay. Whether it is through a flyer, magazine or a trusted friend, when any of us seeks out spiritual classes, they should be informative and worthwhile to our progress, not our detriment. What most people are not aware of is the energetic factor that is created when each of us leaves a classroom. We connect on a cellular level, and because of our common goal and interests, sometimes even bond together for a time after. Even while reading this book you are connected to me, and if you haven't left my company from boredom already, you are most likely learning from the same teachers I learned from. Workshops offer us assistance, practice and tools. People work with each other just hoping to interact with the teacher or master. If we create our intention ahead of time, we can be guided by a Divine Being and make an even better connection with the one teaching us. In actuality, that can also help the teacher be more fluent and aware!

Praying: Be Careful What You Ask For

When praying before or during one of these teaching sessions, we have to be careful not to put a psychic spin on it by attaching an intention that would only benefit ourselves. Asking for the most beneficial outcome for all should be our focus. Also, if the prayer is done while in a state of fear or distress, it is most likely not attached to divinity. If someone is zealous about praying for our advancement or healing, we should ask them who they are connecting themselves to. Is it a Divine Being such as Jesus, St. Francis, Kwan Yin, Krishna, an ArchAngel, and Almighty God? If not, then you may want to politely refuse prayers from them. A dedicated disciple to a guru might offer prayers to whom they believe is their teacher or higher being. A false God or a guru is not a Divine Being, and praying to one can be harmful. Unless we know a person praying for us is absolutely attached to a Divine Being, we are better off praying for ourselves. If you are somehow led to pray to a guru, realize that it will probably act as an energetic attachment between the guru, yourself and the person you are praying for, but for safety purposes, you can ask to attach this guru to a Divine Being.

Some prayer requests are more challenging than others. For instance, when we pray for a loved one who is sick, we create an energy of urgency. We become attached to the outcome, which can skew our sensibility. We start asking questions like, "Is my prayer going to work? Since I didn't go to church every Sunday, am I still worthy of having this prayer answered? What should I be praying for?" Remember that prayer is an intention that creates energy. Ask for the best outcome for all and be prepared for that outcome to not be what you believe is best, but instead what is best in the 'eyes' of God. It helps to remember that God doesn't keep score, nor is God standing by to judge us. (God doesn't have to. We do a great job of that all by ourselves!)

Also, consider that worthiness is not based on what we have or haven't done. It is based on what we are willing to do going forward. Everyone is worthy of healing! There are different types of healing though. There is the physical, the emotional, the mental and the spiritual aspects of being human to consider. We also have to accept that sometimes death is healing. That is difficult to hear, but when you think about how glorious it is to be with our Angels here on earth, imagine what it must be like with them in their domain? For all we know, death may be the easiest thing we do in our lifetimes! We might want to ask these questions: Why all the pain and suffering while we are here? Why isn't there an easy rescue or healing when we ask for one? My belief is that it is because we are only human and not Divine Beings. We are here on earth to resolve and to experience every possible scenario of growth. Why else would we be here? After all my years with the Angels, I am convinced that we are just doing our thing here till we can get there. And we make life here harder simply because we see with a small mind and from a perspective that suits us for that moment. We don't want to see the bigger picture if it takes us away from what we need and want right now in the little picture. And this notion is apparent in all people, those on a spiritual quest or not. We will always be human while here, so we are prone to all human tendencies.

Understanding Bonding

It usually feels good to connect with like-minded people in a New Age workshop, especially since New Age philosophies make most people feel uncomfortable. With those like-minded individuals, however, expect the unexpected. Surprise! There are lots of different energies to connect with...ones that feel good and others that don't. Because they are like-minded people, we might want to assume we would want to bond our energies with them too. I wouldn't be too quick to do that though. With each of us having our own monkey, our own issues, ambitions, fears, limitations and such, each class could proffer an opportunity to take on as much stuff as we are trying to rid ourselves of! It is great that most of these classes are filled with people on the journey of self discovery, but we have to be continually aware of what issues we are exposing ourselves to. The more connected we are to the process, the more connected we can become to the people offering the lessons, the people in attendance and the techniques being offered. Don't consider it too much of an issue though. The cause and effect, whether negative or positive, can be managed.

For instance, if someone were to bond with their teacher or guru, they might enlist all the limitations they feel about themselves and all of the reasons they can't be like the guru. The bond could trigger a memory of being a guru at one time and the karma attached to that experience will begin to express itself. It can also express a history of past lives between the student and the guru, and with that would come all the emotions and belief systems on a conscious and unconscious level. Every bonding has a specific story to tell, and that story runs through us 24/7 until we decide to cut the bond off.

When I speak of bonding, I want to reiterate that it is an ethereal connection between people that expresses itself on a human level. Although we are all soulfully and spiritually connected to each other and to source, our human bonds can amplify our issues and shortcomings. Sometimes they present themselves as cords. Cords are energetic and ethereal attachments between ourselves and another. They represent issues we need to resolve here on earth. So therefore, it is good to objectively look at all our attachments as learning experiences and act accordingly. When I come across people who are in distress because of a relationship with a family member, boss, coworker or anyone they have been or are in contact with, I will help them recognize it as a karmic bond. Once they realize that cutting the other person out of their lives physically did not resolve their issues with them, I can get to work with helping them cut those attachment cords. Cords and bonds will remain forever too unless we cut them, but once we do, it is forever! What once used to trigger these people and leave them powerless and struggling to understand, is now gone and the relationship improves or becomes a non issue.

Divine Beings allow this bonding, by the way. Suffice it to say, we commit and agree before coming to live in human form to the type of lessons we will encounter. Therefore we bond with the specific people needed to instigate these lessons so we can grow. They are like the actors playing their roles in our lives. Divine Beings encourage these relationships, but they are also the only ones that can actually release us from them. Through God, Divine Beings, special prayers and often with the help of a practitioner, bonds, cords and karma can be sought out, found and healed. It is also important to note that we as humans are not going around purposely doing this bonding. Although, it should be noted that there are a few deliberate psychic attachments that can occur, but these are more easily taken apart.

Karmic bonding coincides with our spiritual growth. As we yearn for more healing and awareness, our 'lessons' are revealed. Our bonding history relates to our positioning in spiritual development and offers an opportunity of discovery, then release. We cut bonds and we cut off patterns, eventually clearing our way to enlightenment. Cutting these cords and clearing karmic debt are procedures everyone can utilize for a better, happier life.

Free Passes Don't Exist

I intentionally sought out education and study for my own growth and also to help others. Spiritually speaking, though, I believe I was led to much of my education so I could resolve my own inner conflicts and further my journey here as a healer. It was very natural for me to connect to The Divine during all of it, although in the beginning, I wasn't as aware of how profound a connection I had. Most of us want this connection, and it is our right to do so, but like most, I thought I had to be pure to seek God's help. As awareness increased, judgment of myself decreased and that made it easier to ask for help and guidance.

Whether we are connected to source or not, though, no one gets a free pass. Our stuff doesn't disappear without us doing the work. We need to courageously shed the layers we hide behind in order to reveal truth. We have to say no to the temptations of the ego. My ego expressed itself in a very specific way. I wanted to be known, although I hid this intention very well. It took me many years to resolve the block I had, because I just didn't want to admit to the longing. That kind of ego-energy doesn't belong in the heart or head of a healer. It may be enticing at times to be recognized for our gifts, especially when they are actually helping people. We as humans require validation, but we can't seek it from others. We are only encouraged to ask The Divine for validation of our worthiness and specialness. I tried to cover my need and thought that being humble was more appropriate and conducive to growth. I could have faked modesty forever, but energy doesn't lie. I eventually had to stop *acting* humble and actually start *being* humble.

The law of attraction always plays a role in reminding us what we are not healed from, as our energy expresses itself time and again through circumstance until we change what is emanating from us. The things we resist will persist, and we will see the energy replicated in the people around us. And this is a necessary replication too, because all things we need to rid ourselves of need to be acknowledged and cleared. How else would we know our issues, especially the ones we have hidden from or have run from for years? Sometimes, we need to have pain, discomfort, uneasiness, and anger in order to get moving. Other times we just need to get disgusted with situations or ourselves. "Enough already!" should be our mantra statement, because the sooner we get to know the truth, the sooner we get to heal from it.

Who Am I, You Ask? Well, I am Kiros!

In Greek, there is a saying that goes, *"Show me your friends, and I'll tell you who you are."* At that time, I was surrounded by plenty of people that could give me hints about who I was as a man. One year, I decided to go to every event, ceremony and seminar I could find. I spent countless hours in search of 'me' in these workshops and initiations. Knowledge was my ambition, but recognition was my motive. So many of the people I associated with during this time were what I can describe now as ego driven, needy and prideful. The most competitive group of people I have ever met to date! As much as I can describe them though, what does it say about me?

It was a year full of self-discovery. I really thought that if I could gather with other fellow seekers, healers, practitioners, etc., that I would benefit. The Reiki practitioners were, and still are, dear to me, but Reiki isn't enough to eradicate all our issues. I felt the need to be boundless, but I was unsure of how far I could go and what I was capable of. I had no idea what I could become. Everyone at that time was giving themselves a special name. I had friends who called themselves names like, White Horse, Blue Sky, Thea, etc. My given name, Peter, in my estimation was not a name for a potential healer...someone who could reach greatness. My ego chose "Kiros," because it sounded much cooler and that was how I envisioned myself.

Coming into my 'Power' as Kiros

Since the tapping episode with Cathy during her Reiki session, a lot of other supernatural events occurred. Reminiscent of my calligraphy episode back in Greece, I took to automatic writing and channeling. My hands started to move differently while performing Reiki as well. They resembled a conductors, except my orchestra had no instruments other than energy. At first both hands were synchronized, but that changed, and one started to stir energy while the other moved independently to energies that were surging around it.

The results I had with this new energy movement made me thirst for more. I wanted to know why it was happening, and also I wanted to show off my great discovery. The only people I could find who were willing to listen without judgment were the people who had the same limiting conditions and beliefs. At first, I thought I was studying with a metaphysically elite group. Something didn't feel right though. My gut told me they might have been just as goal driven as me. Instead of listening to my gut, I blindly followed for a while. Once I got my bearings, I took to research, which I find is always the right approach. I needed to give discernment a chance. In accessing my intuition, I could better assess my direction. My Guides would be able to tell me if these were actually situations I could grow from or setbacks. We should always want to stop, ask and listen. Why look back at the magnitude of our setbacks when we can look forward at the beautiful journey without anxiety or fear of the direction we are headed in?

After seeking divine guidance, I realized I was creating a major setback. A lot of the work I was following was being channeled and included general information and training. There was some decent energy activation, but what a flashy doorway I needed to walk through to get to self actualization. I can laugh about it now, but back then I was unnecessarily struggling. As much as my gift could be considered special, we are all special and gifted, so there was no need for a red carpet. Instead of connecting with others based on pure intention and goodness, we became bait for a whole bunch of astral beings who were manipulating us so they could have access to our energy 24/7. Astral Beings are entities that exist in another realm (Astral Plane) between Earth and Heaven. A Lower energy entity (someone who has had human experiences and is still bringing those experiences here through a living person) could offer plenty of research and general information...even healing. A name that comes to mind is John of God, who describes in his book how he channels a group of entities who claim they were doctors in previous lives. Someone that offers physical healing to clients and then allows themselves to be open to whatever guidance may be there to help facilitate, may also be asking for trouble. It leaves the door open for any entity to come forward, especially if they lack experience working in the psychic realms and are not aware of the consequences.

My experience in that year though, with all the teachers and healers I encountered, brought me back to intuition. Only with a higher intelligence and guidance can we avoid the lower energies and teachings. And if we do seek out answers from another Earth guide or teacher, we need to ask them where their information is coming from. If they are channeling it, it is most likely from an astral source and not divine source. As long as the channel is encouraging self-empowerment and the potential for growth, we can feel reasonably safe taking the help and information. If instead it is making one feel powerless and worse than before, consider it coming from a negative source, and don't accept it. Specifically ask anyone you work with, most especially a hands-on healer, who they are working with. If they are not working with a Divine Being and God, then most probably they're working with astral beings.

Lower Energies vs Higher Beings

If we were to go to a practitioner who is channelling an entity, we might wind up paying for it with more than our money. We would actually be contributing our energy to them as well. In order to stop this energy drainage, we might actually need another practitioner who works in a higher astral realm in order to be able to clear it. The astral realm consists of ghosts, entities, Angels, people who haven't crossed over, celestial beings, e.t.s and others...all existing at a certain level of development. Think of the astral realm as a building with many floors. Each astral being is capable of occupying the floor they have evolved to. Some beings may have gotten to the 7th floor, but don't even know an 8th, 9th or 15th even exists. They may not have the desire to leave the 7th or have the fortitude to get to another level. Some may know the next floor exists and are readying themselves for the next level, but aren't ready to take on the next human (earthbound) experience in order to elevate themselves. The Divine is not a part of the astral realm. It is in a realm all its own, however, Divine Beings can go to any floor and beyond. To make it even easier to understand, there are three realms; the one that we exist on known as earth, the astral, and then The Divine. We as humans have access to all three and that is what makes it so awesome to be human.

All of this leads to one conclusion. We need to work with a practitioner who connects to Divine Beings. The astral is more easily accessible because it feeds to our wants and needs. Only Divine Beings can bring us to truth and awareness. We have to be open to what they consider the right path, though, which may seem difficult and not necessarily one we would want to go on given the choice. Essentially, when we are not motivated to go the right way or we are looking for quick fixes and answers, the astral is right there to accommodate us. Understanding the realms and the levels that exist within them, it makes sense that a practitioner would need self realization and a strong conviction to connect with The Divine.

ArchAngels and Ascended Masters are Divine Beings that can access any realm at any time and without having to lose their essence of divinity. Not so, though, for an astral being, which eventually would have to elevate its consciousness. Even if a loving astral being, such as an Angel, is inspired by The Divine, it is still dwelling in the astral. Suffice it to say, though, it would exist on a much higher level than an entity that isn't divinely inspired. If you would like to feel a sense of the energies that are emitted from a divine source versus an astral, try this exercise with a safe astral being such as your Guardian Angel. First, take in a deep breath to clear your senses. Then, ask for your Guardian Angel to join you by saying, "My Guardian Angel please be here with me now." Allow yourself to experience the merge (of energy) for a few seconds, and then when you are done getting a feeling or impression of your Guardian Angel, then ask for ArchAngel Michael by saying the same. "ArchAngel Michael, please be with me now." You should be able to feel a subtle or perhaps significant difference. Your Guardian Angel has been there since the beginning of your existence, so their energy will feel familiar. As far as ArchAngel Michael goes, well all I can say is, he's just magnificent! Afterwards, be sure and thank them both for making their energy known to you.

We shouldn't feel anxiety about being in the presence of the ArchAngels. Divine Beings are here to assist us in our human evolution and growth...teaching us how to access the tools that are already installed within us. These tools are the gifts of our soul (located in our chakra system) and at our disposal anytime we need to access them. This is, so we can live our best human experience and be more unified with God. We should be taking advantage of The Divine interaction that is offered.

"Reality is not just the physical world; it's the relationship of the mind with the physical world that creates the perception of reality. There's no reality without a perception of reality."

—FRED ALAN WOLF

Gratitude

Angels watch over us at all times and protect us from harm. They are God's gift to us and a way to connect with God in times of need, especially when we can't seem to connect on our own. Most of us ask for God's help when we feel desperate. Angels will always be able to listen to our cry of help because they're created for us and are very close within our immediate reality and awareness. I believe Angels are a reliable source of connection and transmitting. Asking for their help is equal to asking God, since they are God's messengers. It helps to think of Angels as humans without egos, filled with love and without negative emotions and limitations. After all, they are not confined to a very fallible human body. Because they are coexisting in our sphere of influence, they help guide us to God. When they need to come to our rescue, it is always divinely inspired, or shall I say, the will of God.

A few years after the snowmobile incident, the Angels had to save me once again. On this particular night, I was driving home after being out with friends. I wasn't drunk, just tired and sleepy. I should have pulled over and slept an hour or so in my car, but instead I pushed myself, thinking it was only ten more minutes to get home. Before I realized it, I fell asleep at the wheel, but when my eyes were forced opened by some ethereal light (almost as bright as the sun), I regained my focus in time to see a concrete wall in front of me! My Angels knew what they were doing. They (the light) woke me up with a zap of energy in just enough time for me to swerve to safety. That was the first and last time I would ever drive tired again. I couldn't sleep for the rest of the night and the next day no matter how much I tried. I think that jolt was equivalent to thirty cups of coffee. Just like the snowmobile incident, though, it didn't prompt my childhood memories of my time with the Angels. Nevertheless, I knew and felt God was behind that rescue. I will never forget how overwhelming that light was...a magnificent, colorful glow. I'm not sure how long I was asleep, but I still remember it now as a visual indication of The Divine.

The more gratitude we have toward the Angels, the more we open ourselves to receiving their guidance and love. We should be thankful for all the time they are around us and not just for the rescues. In addition, the Angels want to give us more, but we need to ask for their assistance. The more we receive, the more we are open to giving as well. So when they give to us, it magnifies their efforts. Angels are love, and the more we interact with them, the more we love ourselves and others. We need to make it a practice to thank God and the Angels every day. It should not be any different from asking our parents or loved ones for help. We have to get it through our heads that they don't have our human limitations and are boundless. They have no time constraints and help everyone simultaneously, so there is no need to worry about taking away from others who need help. I hear it all the time from people, "I don't ask because they are busy with more important things. Others have greater needs than me." Everyone is equally important, and perhaps people are in grave need because they have yet to learn how to ask for help! I am happy to report that asking is appropriate at all times for everyone, irrespective of their perceived worthiness.

Even if all humanity asked for help all at once, ArchAngels would be with every single one of us that asked, and the help would be instantaneous. Isn't that remarkable? It is no different from our analogy of the sun. As long as we are facing it, we are all getting the same attention from it. The same can be said for asking. In order for us to receive their help, we need to ask for it; we need to do it all the time, and we need to do it simultaneously with consistent gratitude. Remember that if we wait to give gratitude till after we receive, we may not receive! Having gratitude before we receive means we expect the best outcome. By asking consistently, we get in the habit of letting go of our issues as opposed to holding onto them. And lastly, as soon as we ask for angelic presence, it helps to lessen the drama we are experiencing. These are such great reasons to ask, but many of us wait so long to do so. Perhaps it is because we don't feel worthy to receive angelic help. Maybe it is because we believe our drama is too big for a Divine Being to handle. Or it could just be that when we are immersed in our drama, we aren't capable of tapping into that part of ourselves that knows there is more to connect to. In any event, Angels are always there waiting, and for that, I am grateful.

"The eye with which I see God is the same eye that sees me. My eye and the eye of God are one eye, one vision, one knowledge, one love."

—MEISTER ECKHART

Early Impressions of Faith and God

Growing up in Greece as a devout Christian and attached to the orthodox church, my faith and beliefs were constantly challenged. Our family wasn't strict about church law, but we still followed traditions. Because our entire nation was involved, all the holidays and traditions were important. It was impressed upon us, and being impressionable, I believed in what I was being taught about God, God's enemies and the enemies of our country. While in high school, attending church was mandatory, and we had to take religious instruction every Saturday at church. There were many icons displayed there. The ceilings were full of images of Saints, ArchAngels, Jesus and other Angels. I loved looking at them, although even their beautiful images couldn't keep me occupied for three hours of service. Church was like a test of endurance for the mind and body. From the sermon and liturgy that was purposely written to scare us, to the long and exhausting ritual of standing on our feet, it was specially designed to wear us down and break our resistance. I imagine they believed that was the only way the Holy Spirit could take over. It wasn't working for me or my fellow students. We all hated going to church on Saturdays. We were forced to remain motionless and so too was our spirit...stuck between darkness and light. There was no escape from the boredom, or the confusion from adults that professed life would be better if we became more dogmatic and disciplined. There was no autonomy, no independence, and eyes were always on us. The Angels peered from the ceiling, Jesus stared with marble eyes from the corner of the room, and the teachers glared at us from the pews.

Under these conditions, no one would ever be purposely disobedient. Well, almost no one. Trouble would find me, even in the house of God.

Can you imagine getting kicked out of church? Leave it to me. It didn't take more than a giggle that turned into a loud chuckle that eventually broke out in a chain of laughter with all my classmates involved. For obvious reasons, the service ended, but not without sneering glances from the priest and officials. Eventually we were escorted out. Even some teachers that laughed got in trouble. In a fear based religious country under the realm of a military dictatorship, this was unacceptable behavior.

It wasn't until I was older did I realize why I felt so uncomfortable in church. I believe now that I understand what being an empath is. I was picking up on negative energies, most especially hypocrisy. It was obvious that much of the congregation would commit sins, then go to church, light a candle, and then believe it was atoned. The bigger the sin was, the bigger the candle that was lit. They would bow and bow and bow some more. I never got to see beyond the humble bow, but I did get to hear all the gossip and stories that led up to the offense.

The Contenders

There was a couple that used to have major fights so often, we called them "The Contenders." One day, I saw the husband in church lighting a huge candle (no surprise), but when he turned around I was shocked to see his huge black and blue eye. Sometimes stress makes us laugh or maybe I just thought it was hilarious, I don't know, but I just started laughing once again. Of course that generated its own drama, and before long, I was being addressed by an angry priest over the loud speaker. It was this kind of event that kept me from wanting to attend church. Whether I was being called out as a trouble maker or tattled on, I was usually escorted out. Eventually our school was not welcome at our local church, so we had to start attending another in a neighboring town.

Is Everything in the Hands of God?

Despite not liking church, I gleaned what I could from the lessons and God's presence there. What I learned is that we can't rest in the expectation that everything is in the hands of God and the Angels without taking responsibility for how our life is being directed. As an example, if someone is in an abusive relationship and the whole universe is telling them to move on and they don't, it is most likely because they are not willing to listen or do the work necessary to get out. They might reach out and ask for support to cope with the abuse, but it would be obvious that they were not willing to make a move to get out of the situation or they would do so. When we are ready, we listen. Before then, God and the Angels stand by with unconditional love and support, always there for us the instant we decide to move forward.

When we look at someone suffering from physical and verbal abuse (most especially if it is being dished out by someone who professes to love them), we might be led to think God doesn't have a hand in it, or worse, that God is allowing it. God's hand is always present, but God doesn't put the abuse there. It is the opposite. God is there to take it away and, most likely, God was there prompting us to never go in that direction in the first place. Thy will be done, but we have to ask for God's Will! In this case, the weakness in one person was the perfect match for the aggressiveness of the other. It paints a picture of suffering and loss of connection between the human self and the soul and therefore, God. A huge lesson for me: There is no salvation unless we ask for it.

People question God's presence, because when they are not looking upon the light, they can't see the light shine upon them. They ask, "If God is the creator of our soul, why would we, as God's creation, be allowed to suffer this way?" It would seem a valid point, but when we look at the creation of a soul and its expression as it exists here and now (in its current human form), there is a huge gap between each experience that has accumulated and the original creation. Spirit is pure within each beautiful soul and continuously expresses love and grace. I believe it always remains pure through eternity. It is the soul that makes us question what is really going on. I really believe that every soul has a beautiful beginning with lots of light and love to share. I think of it as a happy, loving, radiating baby, and we have all experienced how awesome a new baby's presence is.

What if a spirit doesn't want to leave the heavens though? This questions makes me think that there is the potential for it to only partially download into a soul. My best guess is that every time there is a life created in the infinite universe, spirit shows up and takes part in its evolution. Eventually, in time, spirit will assist in evolving that life and bring it back to Source or withdraw from that life and express itself onto another that's also being created. If a spirit has infinite potential, it can be in many creations at once. Now what happens in between a spirits appearance here and its farewell is the mystery and science of life. If we think about Wayne Dyers lesson, which is that we are really spiritual beings having a human experience instead of human beings trying to have a spiritual experience, than we should be able to continually feel our deep sense of connection to everything, most especially Source. Source is everywhere and ever-present irrespective of how we are participating in our soulful/spiritual life. Even if all we aspire to be is sincere and faithful in all our interactions... not wishing to harm anyone in the process of living our life or obtaining our goals...we will be connected. We take it even further by always being thankful for everything we have and helping to teach everyone around us how to create the same connection for themselves.

"Love the moment, and the energy of that moment will spread beyond all boundaries."

—Corita Kent

It Takes a Greek to Know...

Even though I had lost my early childhood memories of the Angels through my teens and young adult life, I always kept the inner knowing that they existed. All I knew of God was from the bible. Like everyone else who is coping with one thing or another, I sometimes asked for help. Sometimes I didn't. Life was always very busy, and most especially when my family moved to New York from Greece. Thirty-five years later, and I'm still counting in Greek and challenging myself to conform to an American existence, which is so vastly different from Greek life. (Think, "My Big Fat Greek Wedding" and you will get the picture.) It was very difficult to meld into this life while the family was acting as if we were still in Greece. "What's wrong with you? Get married!" they would say. "Have babies! Eat, don't think. Just eat! Did you eat? Eat!"

Coming from an ancestry of awe-inspiring philosophers, poets, orators, inventors, sculptors, engineers, heroes, and scientists, I found in comparison that most modern Greeks I was meeting in New York seemed dense and not forward thinking. All of them thought highly of themselves for originating from people like Socrates, but ask them about Socrates' work and many couldn't give more than a sentence or two. The undisputed and valuable work of these amazing men; Socrates, Plato, Homer, Sophocles, Archimedes, Aristotle, Pythagoras, Democritus, and the others should have inspired all of us to learn more. There were fellow Greeks through the years that I could converse with, but most conversations fell short. Sharing some constructive opinions is always good (except for politics, especially with all the of turmoil back in our homeland), but I wanted to have a deeper, more meaningful conversation about enlightenment and self development. If our Greek ancestors could talk, they would be telling us that we need to extricate the lessons they were trying to teach us and discuss them. "With all the information we left for you to read and study, you still have nothing to talk about?"

A native Greek is fortunate to live surrounded by mountains, water and amazing air that offers a clearer spiritual connection to these great minds than we could expect to find here in America or really anywhere else on Earth. There is something magical about Greece that no matter where anyone travels in the country, its essence can fill them up. Whether sitting on a balcony, going for a short walk or sipping coffee at a local bistro, every nuance feels accommodating. There is a strong sense of creative energy as well. It is expressed in everything, even in the unique style of homes for example. It is as if each house was a self portrait. Stimulating, creative and empowering, this environment generates an energy that encourages a free spirit.

I believed for years that the people of Greece would eventually reconsider the decision to take on the European Union's model. Greece and its inhabitants are too inherently different to fit into another type of lifestyle, no matter how much it is being forced upon them. At the time of this book's publishing, it is 2015, and my prediction has been verified. When I go back for visits, I find it so refreshing to hear and feel the passion native Greeks have about life. I recognize it as a boundless free spirit. It is not evident in those of us that have moved to the US. I am not trying to compare cultures either. It has to be partially about the land and environment, otherwise, those that have left having grown up with the same culture, would never lose this passion. When leaving Greece, people seem to have the need to conceal instead of investigating truth. In America, it is more expected to take sides instead of understanding each other's opinion. If anything, what the Greek ancestors taught us and is perhaps a forgotten understanding, is how to break barriers and limitations. Their teachings always encouraged liberation of the soul. Perhaps it is human nature to sometimes want to distance ourselves from any understanding of spirituality left by our ancestors. It is easier to be passive and remain dormant than to stimulate the mind to become more than flesh. Maybe it is all fear driven and that is a shame, because underneath all of it, a tremendous emptiness seems to exist.

And what do any of us do to compensate? Live an exterior life trying to acquire happiness and 'greatness' through personal gain.

Doing Business

Everything that is gained in the physical life is gained by taking. We call it "doing business," and it's considered smart to interact in a businesslike fashion with one other. Integrity sometimes gets in the way of conducting business. We would expect a person to want to activate a trait like integrity, an attribute derived from the soul. Wouldn't anyone want to utilize a beautiful gift of the soul to gain power? And wouldn't we be getting so much spiritual help in doing so? Instead, we see people trying to gain power by lying, cheating, stealing...whatever means necessary to gain what they think they want for themselves. What could possibly come of such a human exchange of energy?

Most of the world believes in some kind of higher power, and they will seek out religious instruction because they want more spiritual growth. Some will go to church or synagogue out of fear or guilt. Others attend to keep themselves holy or faithful. Different faith traditions through time have inspired believers to separate themselves from each other, and man has a long history and a long list of consequences attached. There are people that profit from this long list of conflicts, and in the struggle, humanity has to find its place. As humans, we create many offenses against one another. Although we have leaders and presidents who perpetuate the protection of our allies, we don't necessarily have anyone protecting humanity as a whole. When it comes to war, I frequently ask, "Is any killing humane? For the sake of universal brotherhood, can we see another way out?"

Last time I checked, a mother living in the eastern part of the world will bear a child in the same manner as another in the western hemisphere and equally so up north and down south. The sons and daughters of these mothers are equally loved by a higher power we call God, irrespective of where on the map they reside. Even when they grow up and follow different traditions and faiths, including ones that exclude God's existence, God's love never stops.

And it is not about the big candle either ...

Another question I frequently ask, "Is God needy?" We have been taught that we need to give to the church in order to take care of God's needs. Religion promotes a certain way of thinking and acting that limits and disempowers us. We don't learn how to stay connected to God through our own strengths. Leaders of the church preach to us, telling us who we are, how to grow, and how fast, but that doesn't stop so many of us from cheating, stealing, lying, deceiving, killing, and so on. Then those who do commit the sins light the big candle at church on Sunday or donate the big check to be forgiven. Living in this strictly human way doesn't promote more of God's goodness. We are made in the image of God to create and to live free, happy, and unlimited. And we have help to live this life in an extraordinary way! God and the Angels are there to assist us in our transformation into awareness. They will help us resolve the false images we create for ourselves. A key component in this type of personal growth is to have the courage to see our own truth. We need to discover and uncover all that is holding ourselves in negative abeyance. We need to let go of or change out of anything that does not allow us to move forward in love and God's grace. When we do finally ask for our truth, we see much of what we need to do, and much of it starts with the body.

A lot has been changing already in the way of food habits and how we are deciding to eat and take care of our bodies. Twenty-five years ago, I couldn't find any organic produce in supermarkets. Now it is abundant, although there should be more. As we elevate our consciousness, we need less harmful processed foods and more organic natural meats, vegetables, fruits, and grains. Or is it the other way around? In order to bring ourselves to any true level of awareness, we need to be pure of body! It is the age old question, "What came first the chicken or the egg?" When it comes to living a beautiful life, it doesn't matter! Create the intention to be the best you can be, and whatever aspect needs to be worked on first, whether it is the physical, emotional or mental, the next step will become evident. A teacher, a book, a direction, a coach or guide...everything we need comes right to us. All we need to do is follow the path that presents itself.

The Body as Our Temple

As Hippocrates reminds us, "It is our right to be healthy in mind, body, and spirit," and when we move towards this type of wellness, we will become more in tune with our bodies, nature, what we are drinking, eating and breathing. It is so important to honor and respect all of nature, most especially the animals we consume. It is the humane thing to do, and after all, when we eat them, their bodies blend with ours. We need to help sustain our environment, even if that means standing up for what is right even when everyone else is sitting down. We need to lead by example and stay consistent in our beliefs so we can realize worthwhile change for future generations.

It is time science caught up to humanity by introducing medicine that will better accommodate the human body. Supplementation is sometimes necessary to fill gaps and satisfy the body's need to be whole, vibrant, and healthy, but when we take a substance that fixes one problem only to create another, we never achieve true healing. There are remedies that do not alter, but instead balance. We actually prolong illness for profit when we take pills that take away symptoms, but do not heal us. Is it possible to provide medicine that targets the causes of disease and can create a full-spectrum transformation and healing for people? I believe it is possible when everyone creates an intention to heal instead of earn!

Man-made chemicals should not be used in agriculture for the same reasons they shouldn't be used in humans. Foods that are toxic not only cause all kinds of physical health issues when consumed long term, but also create short and long term chemical imbalances in the mind and body. That translates to mental and spiritual imbalances. Think of all of it as energy that can offer goodness or can take it away. Our bodies constantly rejuvenate, and the nutrients from healthy foods and supplements would provide all that is needed for a vibrant body. Vegetables, for example, absorb their minerals from the ground; so if chemicals are used, the broccoli on our plate is filled with the same pesticides. They are also as depleted as much as the soil they came from. All of this interferes with our neurological system, our endocrine system, and every life support system. How can any of this support our connection to God? Our spirituality? Our awareness? It can't! It can only separate us more.

Am I saying that broccoli laden with pesticides can keep us away from God? In a way, Yes! If there is only one message you derive out of this book about your spirituality, understand that it is our human selves that keep us away from Source, not the other way around. Consuming healthy foods will balance all our systems and make them interact the way they were intended to. That not only helps us connect with our higher self and God, it is the only way the connection will happen. Having a clean body gives us the clarity of mind and allows us to fully participate in the joy of being human and alive. Again words from Hippocrates, *"Let food be thy medicine and medicine be thy food."*

It only makes sense to eat what God provided. How can we think we can create better? Especially when better only means more quantity at less cost. When we feed our body, we have to think about how that will feed the spirit. Everything we hold to our mouth should be subject to the question, "Is this good for me and my body or is it not?" With our soul's guidance, we will make the 'right' choice. With that choice, we will have the clarity and good spirits to always do the 'right thing' as humans. We may get lost on our way at times, or even disoriented, doubtful, and filled with emotion, but eventually we will find our path again if we become more mindful of the body that is housing all that 'stuff.' It may be helpful to view our bodies as on loan. Consider them here on lease with a need to take care of them in order to honor the divinity that granted them to us and that exists within us.

"There is an inner knowing within all of us that we're not of flesh alone; there is greatness within each one and in humanity as a whole. The ArchAngels and other Divine Beings are here to support us in our determination to prevail as humans."

—Kiros

Cause and Effect

We have other means of support available to us. While on my quest for knowledge and enlightenment, I bought countless books on philosophy and spirituality hoping to gain a better connection to Source. It was great to read and learn, but it was around my thirties that I felt led to start doing some hands on learning...literally. After meeting my first Reiki teacher, I immediately became interested in learning more, found a class and enrolled. It was during that schooling when I started remembering my early childhood interactions with my Angels and Guides. It was being fostered, in a way, by my fellow students and that teacher. The more comfortable I became with them, the more I remembered.

Looking back on all of my learning experiences, I would say the second most important factor in human advancement is human support! When we start to develop and realize who we are, what our potential is, and why we are here, things can get a little crazy. It is so important to have human guides and people who believe in us, love us and support all the unraveling we need to do. I don't believe in regrets, but if I were to do things over again, I would want to do some of it differently. I recognize that for any one of us to be a great healer, we need to heal ourselves first. Being cleansed of much of our negativity will lead us to even more healthy teachers and guides. Also, healing others without considering our own issues can distract us from what we need to do for ourselves. It feels so good to do good, so we keep doing for others, but we can get lost in the doing. Besides, if we don't heal first, we can eventually burn out, and at that point, we can't do or be good for anyone, least of all to ourselves.

To find clues about what our healing needs are, we can start paying attention to what others that come to us are looking to heal from. This helped me immensely. We attract like situations, remember? It is the mirror everyone always speaks about. As we use our love and determination to help another, we get guidance and energy we can use on them and ourselves. It might seem unnecessary to do it this way, but there is one aspect to human nature that we take for granted: When we are in denial of something, we are in denial of it, so how can we see it? From a healing perspective, our writer D, who is also a wellness coach, would say, "Denial is a terrible thing to waste." What this means is, the very thing we are in denial of is the very thing we need to look at in order to heal, so don't waste denial. Use it! Look at your mirrors. Universal energy dictates that we will attract exactly what we are, what we think and how we feel. This is one surefire way that our issues will present themselves.

To get specific support, it sometimes helps to stick around our teachers for a while. Most of them have 'been there and done that.' They can appreciate our journey and our need to be lifted. They are also proof positive that we are not alone, crazy or weird for having supernatural energy. We need to stay on planet Earth while we are growing spiritually, but we still need to be lifted in a sense. Ethereally speaking, we shouldn't be in LaLa land. We need to stay in the present and not be led by life. Instead we have to remain confident that we are co-creators. To be a healer is not just about being or portraying a space of tranquility, peace, oneness, and all the other good stuff. It is also about creating our purest intention with our clearest focus while honing our tools. We co-create for the purpose of assisting ourselves, other people, and for all of humanity to gain empowerment and awareness through each other's awakening.

"The greatest of all lessons is to know yourself, because when you know yourself you know God."

—CLEMENT OF ALEXANDRIA

"What was meant to be?"

Over the years, I have heard so many people say, "It was meant to be," or "If it is meant to be..." These meant-to-be-rules that they live by, make me ask, "Meant to be by what standards?" Abundance and prosperity is our birthright. How we earn abundance is different for everyone. Even spiritual people have the need for money. Because they are so used to deprivation though, they usually have the need to be cleared or unblocked from this deprivation mentality. We don't have to feel that wanting means that we are also taking. It also doesn't mean that wanting means we can't give it all back someday. So many of us feel shame about money...having it, making it and spending it. As a result, many shut off from money making efforts. A practitioner or teacher, most especially our ArchAngels, can help with these blocks. We just need to ask.

We're all healers in one way or another, and as our soul reflections interact with each other, we learn, grow, and heal together. It sounds so symbiotic to put it this way, doesn't it? In reality, not everyone is interested in healing work or to help one other, and that is okay. No matter where we stand in regard to our personal healing and growth, however, support is key to continued advancement. We all get ourselves in situations where we need advice. Going to friends and family is not always helpful. Professional assistance is sometimes the only way we can get out of our own way.

Filled with ideas and goals, I knew where I wanted to go most of the time, but couldn't always get the motivation to follow through until I started asking for support. I can't emphasize enough how valuable it is to open our minds and hearts to assistance. Simply put, "The more we ask, the more we receive." Most of us would stop and ask for directions if we were traveling and became lost. Think of our life journey in the same way with abundance being our destination. Sometimes we just need directions on how to get there. Do you know anyone who is not looking for abundance of love, joy, happiness, and fulfillment? Most of us seek this out in our relationships, but when things start going sour, we may not ask for guidance. The first thing any of us should do with any issue in a relationship is ask ourselves to see the lessons. Just asking for truth of our own participation will stop an opposing interaction. Ask, "Does this relationship remind me of a previous one?" By inquiring about our own participation, we have also asked for assistance from our Guides and our higher self. When that assistance comes in, it may be in the form of truthful statements we all of a sudden hear in our head; it can be in the form of energy that can take us up and out of ourselves long enough to see the whole picture; it can be in the form of more love energy to push past negative emotions. Maybe it will be in the form of guidance from an outsider, but irrespective of how the help comes in, it will all benefit us, and we deserve it just because we asked for it!

Everything we need to know and do in order to heal and give and share more love will come into us in the form of thoughts, feelings and nudges. And sometimes that feels like more drama instead of help. Fear not, though, because it is all good and necessary to seek out and heal from the underlying issues. It is helpful to remember that a current situation is not only triggering the drama and emotions we feel in the now, but it also acts as a reminder of similar emotions we experienced from the past. A present-day situation gives buried emotions an opportunity to resurface...a way to come out of the closet, so to speak. Everything that is experienced in the conscious mind and in the body can be used as a mechanism to growth, but instead of learning and growing, we tend to keep repeating the same issues without resolving anything.

At the same time, painful emotional experiences that we don't resolve get energetically registered in our chakra system. This is actually helpful though. We can tap into either the mind or the body as resources of information to help resolve any issue if we desire healing from it. Being a certified clinical hypnotist, I saw firsthand how the subconscious mind can retain every detail of an event, even after many, many years. Fortunately, it is not always necessary to get hypnotized to clear blockages. Sometimes, just acknowledging the lesson and what we have learned is enough to create a shift in awareness, allowing for a spontaneous release. Because we usually hide from hurtful issues, hypnosis is a much faster, more effective and supportive course toward realization.

Relationships Revealed

When we first meet someone and feel attracted to them (the operative word being feel), some of this attraction has to do with the chakra systems...theirs and ours. Physical appearances do play their role, but if we were to go back and look at all our past relationships, we would see many of the same scenarios being played out with people who look completely different. This would suggest that we aren't attracting like people for their physical attributes. We are most likely attracting our lessons whether we want to acknowledge them or not. Sometimes, male/female relationships become a continuation of our mother/father connections that have not yet played out. Karmic partners, soul mates, twin flames...

these are names given to describe our connection to lovers and partners. Sometimes we are meant to be with someone to play out karmic debt; other times souls are re-united for our earthly advancement, and then there is the most connected pair called the twin souls. Supposedly, these are souls that were once one form (at the time of creation) and then split apart. There are many books written about these partnerships, but irrespective of what kind of love lesson is being played out in any of these relationships, it can be more easily resolved by asking for divine guidance and assistance.

Unresolved issues can dictate conscious and subconscious conduct. When anger exists within a relationship, it is often a collection of events that create the energy expressing itself, and it doesn't necessarily have to come from the present scenario. One partner can be dumping on the other from their own collection of 'stuff.' Since we create energetic bonds between each other, anger and other emotions can run 24/7 between two people. The more emotional energies are displayed in the relationship (meaning, the more we fight with each other), the more that gets added onto the energy bond! This is one of the reasons why I tell people who are looking for their twin soul or soul mate to also ask for constant support to come with him or her, because they are going to need it!

"We must let go of the life that we have planned, so as to accept the one that is waiting for us."

—Joseph Campbell

A Cycle of Experience

Every experience we have, good or bad, is registered in the subconscious for future reference. Did you ever touch a hot stove when you were young? If so, I'm sure you never forgot and never tried it again. This is more or less the way we process information and also the way we store it. We put everything into categories of what feels good, what feels bad, what gives us pain, what we like and what we don't like. We also learn at a young age how it feels to receive love and more importantly, what it feels like when it is not being given. Everything we experience at that stage of learning and growing creates a lasting impression. Depending on what we are here to do and learn, we will hold impressions that are appropriate for this life experience. You could say we get trained and/or preconditioned early on.

For example, if we had an impression of unworthiness within our subconscious, and it was put there unintentionally at a young age by our loved ones, it would create an energy of unworthiness that projected from us. This energy will express itself in the way we think about ourselves, in the way we feel about ourselves, in our actions and in our verbiage. In addition, we also spoke about what could be projecting from our aura and chakra system, which is energy from the trauma attached to the events that created the unworthiness in the first place. That means that whatever is going on inside of us is what others will feel as energy coming from us. So many scenarios with various emotions and traumas can be played out as examples here, but I don't want to complicate this. Suffice it to say, that no matter what we do or how much we resist this unworthiness, it will persist. We can run, but we can't hide from our own shadow!

This is why many of us repeat the same scenarios over and over and over again. When we are in these cycles, we experience unhappiness, depression, and a general depletion of our energy. It takes a lot to sustain major emotional baggage, not to mention time consuming. Drama is the key word here, and it is fueled by anger, fear, anxiety...all attached to some sort of pain that keeps us from forward movement. But there is help. We can ask God and the ArchAngels for their assistance and guidance, allowing them to show us truth about ourselves, the situation, and the others involved. We can ask to see our participation without judgment of any one. Since there is no fault or blame, there exists only circumstance.

Divine guidance will come in various forms, and that's because we all are unique and will perceive in our own special way. We are also at different stages of awareness and pain. It could come as a feeling of peace, happiness, and joy. It might be presented as a visual in our mind that helps us to understand truth. My client Sara asked for truth in a love relationship that had just ended. There was drug and alcohol use involved, but she didn't want to judge him. Instead, she asked God to help her feel what it was like to be him. Christians refer to this as an "intercession." God allowed her to feel and take on his pain, childhood traumas and depression for 36 hours. "Kiros," she said crying, "I have never felt so full of dread and complete sorrow in my life! I couldn't bear it any longer and begged God to take it away." God did, of course, and she felt physically fine just hours after asking, but emotionally and mentally, she was never the same. Not only did it change her perspective about depression in general, it helped her to see the state he was in without judgment. Her unconditional love for him came to her in full force, and any negative feelings were gone. Eventually, she asked me to release their energy bond, which in this case was a cord of attachment. Of course I did. As a spiritual coach, I understand all too well how our patterns repeat themselves.

It doesn't really matter how we are shown truth. It only matters that we have the willingness to ask and fearlessness to hear. God does the rest. We can trust the who, what, when, where and how things will play out to Divine guidance since Divinity is all knowing and can determine what form guidance will come in, how we will hear it best, and more importantly, what we can handle. No one is innocent, by the way...meaning that we all have participation in getting to where we are. When any of us gets stuck struggling in a cycle of experience and not asking for help, guidance or forgiveness, it is usually because we are not taking responsibility for what went on. Sometimes it is a karma situation, and we have to experience the same pain that we may have inflicted on another person at some time in our life. It is okay to have some resistance when it comes to forgiveness. We are human, and God made us that way. Just take in a deep breath and ask for it anyway. Eventually the ego catches up to the soul or should I say, the soul catches the ego before it can do any more damage!

Denial and drama keep us struggling and unable to let go, but nothing is too big for the ArchAngels to handle. Ask ArchAngel Michael and ArchAngel Raphael to assist you. As soon as you do, their loving and powerful presence will break any resistance or struggle. After all, we are spirits having a human experience, so ethereal energy to ethereal energy has to work! We need to realize that as humans, we won't be able to clear the way to a happy and harmonious life here unless we can let go of the drama. Let's remember that drama is human perception. It may not be based on reality other than the one we have made it into. ArchAngels can help us see clearly. ArchAngels are facets of God, and they each have their unique way of expressing God's love and assistance. They want to help us to love more, so anything we ask in this regard is a welcome assignment.

ArchAngels Personified

ArchAngel Chamuel is the relationship ArchAngel. We can seek this Angel's assistance when we need help resolving relationship issues, finding a job and to locate lost objects.

ArchAngel Gabriel is one of the most well known, because Christians believe that this Angel was the messenger God sent to tell Mary that she would give birth to the baby Jesus. Muslims believe Gabriel dictated the Qur'an to Mohamed. Gabriel can help you establish discipline and order in your life.

ArchAngel Jophiel is the ArchAngel of illumination. We can go to Jophiel when we need help in absorbing information and wisdom.

ArchAngel Michael is the captain of all ArchAngels and all other Angels. We can seek his assistance when we need protection and when we want to remove any negativity. He protects those who travel, as well as police officers, firefighters, and politicians. He is also the protector of church, heaven, and earth. ArchAngel Michael can be everywhere at once, so we don't ever have to feel we are taking him away from other charges. In fact, this is true with all the ArchAngels.

ArchAngel Raphael is the healing ArchAngel. People can request healing of the body, mind and soul for themselves and for loved ones. He supports the healers and encourages them to ask for their own healing, personal growth and transformation in order to be more efficient at healing others. This is also the Angel to go to for physical needs such as food, clothing or shelter.

ArchAngel Uriel is the ArchAngel of salvation and peace. Uriel can help us turn disappointment into victories, find blessings in adversity, and release painful burdens and memories through unconditional forgiveness and love.

ArchAngel Zadkiel is the ArchAngel of mercy and helps us to overcome sin, allowing us to move forward in healthier ways. Zadkiel also helps us remember what is most important so we can focus on what matters most in life.

It is essential to know that ArchAngels are Divine Beings who love to work with people. So don't be shy about asking the ArchAngels for guidance, healing, and support for your personal transformation. It's very simple. Just say out loud or softly, "ArchAngel Michael, be here with me now, for I need to be safe, assisted, protected, supported..." Explain to ArchAngel Michael why and how you need help, and that's all. As soon as you mention an ArchAngel's name, they are instantly there with you. Also, remember to offer gratitude. A thank-you will do just fine.

"And in my experience with thousands and thousands of people, I've seen that down inside the soul and the human heart of the individual is a core of radiant love."

—John F. Demartini

The Cause of Drama

My mantra for the last few years: "To search and find the happy self...the one free of stuff...the unlimited person inside." That's how everyone seems to feel after a clearing and when all the drama and residue of such has been removed...a little closer to that person within. I get calls all the time from people who are under so much pressure from one thing or another that is taking them away from their inner self, their potential and happiness. There is some validity in all experiences and struggles, but when we look deeper to the cause, we begin to understand the effect. At each session, I listen to what the person is saying about the havoc a situation is instigating, and it would seem very convincing, but I know better. Only when we dig deeper under the drama do we find the real cause. The effect that presents itself is only the symptom of whatever we need to heal from. Even though I am not a therapist, I sometimes have to listen to stories in order to gain some perspective. Truthfully, I don't want to hear the drama. It confuses the process. I offer spiritual solutions through energy healing, so it would make sense that I don't need to know the gory details. I leave that to the therapists!

The effect we have on one another can be blatant and obvious, because, unless we heal from the cause, it will never de-activate, and therefore the effect will never recede. For this reason, however mild something starts out, it becomes worse over time. Potentially, the struggle can become bigger than the relationship and can take the focus away from truth and reality. One issue can also cause all other aspects of life to seem more troublesome. The complaints I hear often include work, relationships, money, family conflict, depression, anxiety, and fear. All are justified concerns and issues, but from my experience, I know there is always more to tell than what I am hearing. I usually put out a blanket statement to everyone: "Let's wait and see what the ArchAngels have to show us."

Clients argue all the time that they already know what is going on. I tell them, "That's good, but why not ask them anyway?" Most people want to leave their focus on the drama and conflict and not to what may lie under the surface. When focusing on the who did what to whom, they can distract themselves from what is really going on. Blame takes all the responsibility off of oneself and puts it on the other. I try to get people to refocus on their own participation. When someone is reaching out beyond their comfort zone for support, it is because drama has been taking them away from their truth, and they need to be redirected towards it. Drama didn't fix anything up to this point. Drama is going to continue to keep them away unless I help them put an end to it. By the time someone comes to me, they are serious about getting rid of this negativity in their lives. Asking for help on this level is a solid step towards ultimate healing from the never-ending, do I have to say it again, drama!

Spinning in The Drama Cycle

One day I got a call from Tracey. She was very upset, and I could tell immediately, she was in drama mode. I politely explained to her that focusing on just the drama is not going to help and that my job is to discover what is causing all the angst in the first place. She replied, "Well, it is obvious it is my manager," and then she went on to tell me how her manager is selfish, inconsiderate and unfair to her and everyone at the office. She also said this manager didn't do any of her own work and made others cover for her. She showed up late every morning and always left early. Tracy howled, "Her lack of responsibility is infuriating! All her frequent displays of incompetence…she's getting away with everything, because no one is holding her responsible. We complain and no one listens! How can someone on that level of management be that irresponsible and get away with it!"

The rantings were generating emotions ranging from anger and frustration to resentment and bitterness. The whole situation was also causing some physical discomfort with her stomach and back. She had a ton of support too, but unfortunately it was supporting her bellyaching, not her healing. Since everyone at her workplace felt the same way about the manager, she had more reason to hold onto the negativity. She also felt more justified. Tracey wasn't ready to let go...yet. She had enough resolve and desire to call me though, so her intention was there. She listened to me with reserved hesitation as I tried to give her another perspective, but it didn't penetrate her resolve. After that conversation, things got worse for her. They usually do when we are at the crossroad, meaning; we are being shown a new way to go, but we stay on the current path or choose another that may actually be more difficult. About a month later, she phoned, and I could tell by her voice that she was ready to hear truth and to let go of whatever she was holding onto. As always, I asked the ArchAngels to assist and guide us, and to make sure that I didn't put my energy into it, I asked to stay neutral.

It didn't take long for the ArchAngels to show me why Tracey was so upset with her manager. It had to do with emotions that were stored deep inside from long ago. The manager's behavior was triggering the memory of another person that had a big impact on Tracey's teen years, namely; her older sister. Tracey had played the role of mother to this older sister who was totally irresponsible and able to get away with everything. Although Tracey played that role well, she did it with a lot of underlying anger, regret and resentment. Bit by bit, she lost more and more of herself in the role of caretaker. Even though Tracey moved on with her life in adulthood, the cycle of this emotional experience never left her. Now forty years later, she was willing to look at this accumulation of negative emotion and release it.

We can distract ourselves with drama for just so long, but eventually, the emotions created from our cycles of experience (some refer to it as 'emotional baggage') will attack so forcibly, we have no choice but to face them. It is very easy to get distracted and get into the drama of a cycle, because no one wants to look at their participation in getting to a frantic state. Suffice it to say, if we bury pain from the past because we can't handle it, why would we want to bring it back and face it again? It is part of the human experience to protect ourselves in this way. Unfortunately, though, once a cycle is created, more affiliate cycles become attached, making it even harder to face and also harder to expose the real cause. While it stays active and potentially hidden, the cycle resonates the accommodating rhythm of drama for an indefinite amount of time. The emotional triggering of a cycle could vary in its effect, registering as small and relatively insignificant at first, to major and possibly life altering since all our thoughts, concepts and belief systems are attached.

These cycles are capable of changing our perception about everything that happens to us, and as I have already stated, they generate an energetic attraction for more drama. All of this creates an intensity of feelings that can make any situation more dramatic than it has to be. To explain better how this actually works in real life situations, I will create a situation. A person named Bob is recently separated and is looking for a new relationship. Since he is coming out of drama from this failed relationship, there is already heaviness around what he is trying to attract going forward. Bob spends some time looking and is not happy about any of the people he meets. Every one of them lacks the qualities he desires and he is lackluster about each. Underlying the issue of who to choose is his loneliness and a severe need to share love, companionship and intimacy. If we were to observe Bob from the inside out, we would find that his belief system, which is filled with drama and trauma from his past, is supporting and justifying everything that is happening in his life so far. Like most, he puts blame on society, the economy, government, and women in general, but he doesn't take responsibility for any of his own issues, the energy he is projecting or underlying causes. It is easier for him to say to himself, 'They are all the same! They are all needy! There are no good women out there!' then it is to understand that he may be attracting the same woman over and over again so he can work out his own issues.

We could look at Bob's situation and believe that everyone who came into his life was there to support his awareness and growth. What a great way to view each person and situation we encounter! We need to remember that the triggering of our emotional cycles occur so we can be reminded of what we need to bring closure and understanding to. One day I might pray to the ArchAngels and find out whose idea it was to have us grow in life through emotional response! It's a slow process, very disorienting and simply painful. Depending on tolerance levels, it can take a long time to figure out the cause of our triggers. But perhaps that is part of the process. Our perception of pain changes as we become more aware. When we accept that everyone is human and flawed; when we accept that we are all growing; when we stop expecting from one another; we won't have as many issues or drama to worry about.

In this case study with Bob, we see his struggle to satisfy his specific needs. Every woman he meets will come up short, because his needs can't be satisfied by another person. They first have to be addressed and then healed by him. If compatible companionship is desired by Bob, then he needs to understand and expect that the person he attracts will be exactly like himself...needy. Most often, I help people discover that their needs stem from patterns developed early on in life. For some it is a parent, others a rejection from their first love, a teacher or spouse. Any of these situations may create a false image of ourselves and others. It limits our thoughts, ideas and feelings of self worth and esteem. From the moment we experience these losses up until we are willing to face and release them, we do what I have been referring to as 'mirroring.' We attract in others exactly who we are and what we are sitting in.

Rescue

If Tracey or Bob wanted to ask the ArchAngels or God for help, they could have said something like "ArchAngel Michael, God, please show me the truth about myself and what has been holding me back." At that point, they would just need to trust and stay open to receive answers. They needn't worry about how the ArchAngels and God will show them. The Divine know all about Tracey and Bob, their issues and their fears. It always helps to remember that they know us better than we know ourselves. It makes it easier to trust in their guidance. When our intention is to heal, we can't allow our minds to get involved. The mind is what got us in trouble in the first place. We have to try and stay receptive. I like to say, "Stay loose!" as opposed to being rigid, so the direction and information can be received. We can allow for our creative and imaginative right side of our brain to assist. That is where all ethereal messages will arrive.

It helps to write down any thoughts or notions that start to come into your head. If nothing comes in at first, start making things up to get the flow going, and don't be surprised if what you are writing doesn't make sense at first. Eventually, when the mind loosens up, more information starts pouring in, and what is being written will start to resonate. Take the time every now and then to inhale deeply. That helps to clear the mind of scattered thoughts.

ArchAngels see right through us and know exactly what we need to hear in order to heal ourselves and create great change in our personas. When I ask for guidance from them as a facilitator of other's clearings, my intention for each client is to ask for healing of the near, far and present causes. I notice that current situations also relate to past lives. Past-life experiences are important (and this concept warrants an entire book of its own), so I want to mention them here. In short, we need to understand that emotional triggers and lessons in the here and now will generally consist of karma from the past that went unresolved. After the clearing, I always thank the ArchAngels and God for their loving support and devotion. I recommend that everyone do the same.

Broken Record

If we experience a repeat of the same scenario over and over, rest assured, we are not paying attention to the lesson that is in play. All of us will respond in different ways to this. What one person considers a challenge to overcome will give another person cause to blame someone else. Basically, when we have a response that is positive or negative to people and situations, it is because they are registering within our core of identity. This is a human form of expression and acts like a holding and releasing system. Each of our emotional reactions creates a unique emotional energy charge that will carry the history of the episode. Over time, these energy charges will condition us, mold our belief system and increase our sensitivity...all adding up to what makes up our human persona. We perceive, respond and react to each future scenario according to how our past emotional charges are expressing themselves. All of this energy exchange is what I have been referring to as 'drama.'

It helps to remember we are co-creators in our lives, which means that everything coming in has been our own manifestation. It is not always done consciously. We often follow our left, very human brain rather than our right, very intuitive brain. Out of habit and comfort we tend to place our awareness aside and rely on our less positive state of mind to direct our verbiage and actions. By acting out the condition our mind is in, we pull in more negative experiences for ourselves and from others. Repeat scenarios should catch our attention. When D and I work together, I hear her ask our clients, "Who is the common denominator in all your life episodes?" Of course everyone answers,

"Me!" If this is true, then it makes sense that all situations are just mimicking what energy we are putting out there. When we see 'faults' in others, we need to look at ourselves. Everyone is our mirror and can reflect back to us who we really are.

With that in mind, we can start to realize an inner reality when interacting with other people. If we only focus on the surface of an issue (what a person is bringing to our current drama), we only see the drama. Dig a little deeper, however, and we find that most people are assisting us by triggering any and all issues we need to heal from. That realization alone alleviates the intensity of the drama! We can also evaluate if a person is a healing agent by how they weaken or strengthen us. Both ends of this spectrum can be a catalyst for change. Extreme emotion is always a precursor for change as well. When we start to feel it and understand its importance as a mechanism to change, we can take the driver's seat and steer toward self empowerment, transparency, emotional freedom and an overall happy life. There is always a lesson and an opportunity within every relationship to gain enlightenment and grow as a person. Whether drama represents an accumulation of 'stuff' we collected in this life or from a past life, doesn't matter. We should focus on this lifetime since it is what we know. It will erase and eradicate all that happened in the past as well. Lucky for us, karma moves backward as well as forward!

Looking in the Mirror

It is pretty much automatic to attach the emotion of anger to a fight or argument, but some of us wouldn't make the connection as easily the other way around. There are times when the feeling of anger created the argument to begin with. There is always a lot more going on behind the scene (or should I say before the scene) of any drama. We either choose to or are driven to respond with emotion, and this emotion can be intense and out of control. It might be more appropriate to say the emotion has control of us and any reasoning. Regardless of whether the storyline makes us feel happy, sad, good or bad, every dramatic episode we experience will eventually register an emotion in the subconscious.

Since our subconscious and chakra system are continuously uploading the episodes of our life, we will continue to be part of the same story/conflict/drama. We become the actors in a play that seems to write itself and longs to be played out, except this play has Act 1 and Act 2 and 3 and 17, 25, 53...it's the play without a finale. Unless we finally decide to draw the curtain, the drama will never end. When we decide to heal from our issues, the drama lessens and sometimes ceases to exist. The opposite is also true. When we disregard the need to heal, the drama increases and each scene in our life drama becomes more intense. Additionally, when we blame our emotional state on everything and everyone else, the emotions will amplify. I can't imagine why all this negativity wouldn't encourage each of us to close that curtain, but I find some people are actually addicted to relationship drama. Whether past lives predicated their 'woe is me' mentality, or they are just too exhausted, unwilling or unmotivated to change, some people just can't seem to break their drama cycles. They are not taking responsibility for attracting or participating in the past or current drama, which will continue to bring in new relationship drama with new partners that have the exact same traits as the previous ones.

When we don't decide to actively heal out of our own 'stuff,' we can expect to see the same familiar scenarios being played out. It could be of equal or greater degree of turmoil too. If we start to take responsibility, we can see less of a degree. If we learn from them as well, we can expect even better results. When old patterns are addressed and re-directed, when self-realization and discovery occurred, then the new relationship experience will express that. There may also be an intrinsic objective in our relationship choices at that point. Whether we understand our lesson or not, as long as we intentionally move forward with the knowledge that we attracted our past woes and we are willing to heal from them, then we will attract a person that will help us learn and heal. It is up to us at that point to actually learn without blame. Self-realization through relationship interaction helps us advance quickly. It is through these give-and-take, unconditional-love scenarios that we can advance in the most positive direction towards happiness.

When we create the intention to love another more than our need to be angry with them, we elevate ourselves as ethereal beings and go deeper into human awareness. With that said, it is important to recognize the intentions of others. Not everyone will have the same intention to love us as we have to love them. They might have the need to protect their drama, so we need to protect ourselves by putting more focus on what they are doing versus what they are saying. When it comes to important choices and life decisions, most of us rely on our feelings, which puts us in tune more with our heart and not our gut. The heart can be overloaded with various emotions though.

A great book that discusses this overload is "The Healing Code," written by Alex Loyd, ND, Ph.D., and Dr. Ben Johnson, MD, DO, NMD. They explain how the heart has as many, if not more, neural peptides than the brain does. That means that it has the ability to carry memory. These doctors describe the memories as pictures we carry with us that can't be released with traditional talk therapy. Each picture can be representative of a big trauma or little trauma and can alter our perception of what is going on at any given moment. So when we allow only our heart to dictate our direction, we can be taking advice from a very confused and injured source. With this information, we can also understand how our entire body can react to any given situation or person, proffering an immediate emotional reaction that we have to try and manipulate our way out of. And we can't discount our ego in this process. When we allow our ego and our need for personal gain to dictate our state of mind, truth becomes even more distorted. The ego supports an energy of justification and allows us to reason with ourselves about our needs and wants. This alone can instigate drama and the need for repeat scenarios.

When we are more interested in personal gain than in living harmoniously and symbiotically, lessons start coming in fast and furious. It is important to always decide whether we are in the giving or receiving end of a relationship and/or a lesson. There is a simple way to tell the difference, too. We just have to check our intentions to know for sure what we are trying to 'give or receive' from each person we meet.

Taking Ownership

Fear of failure, despair, confusion…any and all negative emotions can make us defensive as well as a little stubborn. Feeling these emotions force us to put up walls and possibly deny the need for outside help or advice. More importantly, being in these emotions or a state of denial will block out the actual emotions we need to feel in order to heal. Considering an emotional cycle never leaves us, when we intend to heal, the energy of the soul will eventually work to break down the walls. The more motive we have to change, the faster we see truth about the cycle we are in and what we are in denial of. Drama is a great distraction, but it can only distract a well-intended person for so long before they realize it is damaging and a waste of time. A healthy interaction should play itself out in a reasonably short period with a very deep awareness for all parties involved. In a perfect scenario, both people entering a relationship are trying to grow. The world, though, is filled with imperfect people. In any case, we need each other in order to find awareness. We need other actors to be in our play!

Awareness leads to healing, but it is only the first step. For example, if a wife knows her husband is a narcissist, and she understands she was capable of attracting him, this knowledge alone is not sufficient to clear her triggers. Understanding takes us in the right direction, but it doesn't pack enough awareness of our own issues and self-identity to help us recover fully. Let me offer a scenario as an example of how triggers could play out. My client Linda works in a dental office as a receptionist. On a seemingly good day, a patient named Martha called in to change her appointment. A few minutes with Martha on the phone, and Linda's entire mood changed. It wasn't that she didn't handle the situation or Martha's request. Neither was a big deal. For some reason though talking with Martha created a perceivable shift in Linda's state of happiness. She was aware that she suddenly felt sad and a little angry. She accepted that this new negative expression of energy might have come from the patient, so she tried to shake it off. A coffee latte and donut later, she felt better, and by the time she arrived at home a few hours later, only superficial impressions of a bad mood remained.

An inquisitive phone call from her mother came in later that evening though, and it triggered some out-of-control emotions to emerge. "Did you eat something healthy for dinner?" her mom asked. "What time did you get home?" Just simple small talk coming from a loving and somewhat controlling parent. Linda reacted to it by having an immediate melt down. "Leave me the heck alone!" she screamed, and then threw the phone across the room. Although her reaction seems strong, it is pretty typical of how we store rage. Her mother was not aggressive on the phone, but her questions triggered past behavior that Linda had endured for years. Up to that point, Linda had control of her emotions and refrained from getting into conflict with her mother. On this day, however, a dormant trigger became amplified.

Let's talk about Linda's interaction with her client, Martha, earlier that day. Although I am not offering much information about Martha, suffice it to say that her energy was synergetic with Linda's. They both had mother issues, and these underlying mother issues created a belief system in both of them, which was being expressed through feelings both had about giving and receiving love and acceptance of themselves and others. When someone comes into our lives with similar emotional charges as our own, that person can trigger us. It is just another way of exposing and bringing to the surface all of our hidden and unaddressed issues. Without creating an intention to heal, any of us would try to cover up this type of discovery, finding it difficult to accept. Again, we suppress for a reason. We don't want to resurface hurt feelings because they hurt! In this case, Linda was never nourished by her mother and was longing for it. She had already created an intention to heal from any underlying unhappiness she was experiencing in her life. That triggered the response. The intensity of her desire to heal created the intensity of her reaction. Look at it this way, if we need to wake up, then we need a shake up! We need whatever it takes to move out of the state of complacency and habit we find ourselves in. Right after the phone call from her mom, Linda took responsibility for the entire episode and called me to begin the healing process.

It helps to know that our emotions get triggered all the time. Whether we intend on a human level to grow out of them or not, they will still occur. The law of attraction applies here. In addition, our higher self is always prompting us to move towards growth irrespective of our ego's desire or lack of desire to grow and heal. Like magnets, we get pulled towards one another so we can experience a lesson in hopes of growth. All this happens with the blessing or our higher self, but advancement only comes when our ego makes the choice to do so.

The Reward for Self Recognition

The faster we realize the main purpose of a cycle, the faster we let go, and the faster our life will change for the better. Awareness makes life less confusing and complicated, which aids in the happiness factor.

Once we start to eliminate our cycles, we can feel a new freedom from the people and situations that used to trigger us. We start to have a sense of wholeness that vibrates from our core. As one moves forward and away from the limiting cycles, new opportunities in every aspect of our lives are accommodated by our new energetic pull. That is the law of attraction at its finest. Our energy changes, our minds change along with our future. The decision to be in this state of awareness is so much better than being back in the old self with it's limiting beliefs and crazy drama. Shedding from the old self to the new feels authentic. It is a 'place' filled with clarity, self empowerment, self worth, and love, which makes us feel more alive and joyful. And the happier we feel, the better we function, so why wouldn't we all want to continue that flow?

A spark of awareness allows for new interpretations as well. We realize that people we engage with are clearly connected to our growth in as well as we are a part of theirs. The swift understanding of the role each of us is playing in the world helps to bring a new interpretation of our own suffering. Moving forward, this clarity helps us make better choices and decreases our chances of repeating lessons. We can track our advancement by asking ourselves questions like, 'How am I handling discomfort? Do I run from it or run to it? Who surrounds me now as compared to the past? Are new opportunities coming my way?' Our flow of life becomes more evident. We can feel right away when we are stuck. We are more likely to be honest with ourselves, which will always usher in a non-judgmental assessment of our participation in any situation.

When this level of awareness is reached, we need to be proud of ourselves and the journey we have undertaken. We need to also intentionally send love and compassion to all those in our lives that were instrumental in our growth, whether they were aware of this assistance or not! We can also take a deep breath and relax, knowing the past was only drama needed for our growth. Life becomes fun when we get to choose our point of reference. Learning how to be co-creators in our life should come natural and it doesn't have to be difficult.

"If we have no peace, it is because we have forgotten we belong to one another."

—MOTHER TERESA (1910–1997)

It Is Our Birthright to Be Happy, Free, and Unlimited

Should we blame all of our faults and human tendencies on Adam and Eve? Or maybe we should blame the serpent or the apple itself. It is easier to blame the serpents and apples in our lives, but to accept that we choose to bite the apple is smarter. We need to constantly re-group, reassess, and re-evaluate our actions, asking for guidance and support all along the way. It is really very simple; either one is happy, free, and unlimited, or not. We either feel we are living in abundance or we are feeling deprived. Depending on where in the world we are living, our interpretation of abundance will vary. Even so, no different from Adam or Eve, we have co-created our life experience whether we believe it is a great life or not.

None of us would choose to be somewhere in the world as a starving, deprived child, would we? No, but there seems to be a reason behind suffering. If earth was a place where everyone was in a state of bliss, happiness, love, and joy, we would call it heaven. I believe we as humans can create a heaven-on-earth experience, but instead we write a play and create the drama of un-heavenly behavior. Our precious planet, Earth, is our school. Some of the drama will lead to our greatest growth if we are intending to let that happen. If we don't, it just keeps playing out. Happily, we are still being loved and supported and without judgment from our creator no matter how we choose to behave during our stay here.

When we can mature a little, take responsibility for our deeds and learn to love one another, the possibility of a glorious comeback will emerge. For the sake of human evolution, we need spiritual expansion through self healing and awareness. Just a percentage of us doing this will increase everyone's chance of realizing the same. Then too, there were those who have already been here and done so. For them we should all be thankful.

To Give or Not to Give

Looking back at our own history, we can determine what choices we made that affected others and maybe even harmed them. When we intend for our own gain and success without also intending the same goodness for others, we create an energy that would mimic the same selfishness. This is the law of return. Since we live in a society where everyone wants 'things,' to make them feel good and fit in, we tend to buy brands with famous names on them so people will think highly of us. Many emulate the actions of those they idolize as well. When we do this, we are more likely to push away all sense of our own integrity and morals, thus compromising our own identity. On the flip side, when we identify with people who are generous with their time and money and are powerfully rooted in goodness, we share in the affect they have on our world. Most likely that will lead us to be more generous as well.

Ever try to give to someone who doesn't want to take from you? There are people who are not open to receive, and giving or forcing ourselves on them can cause damage. There is always a reason behind this non exchange too. We can be driven to save the world. That would seem to be an honorable mission. If you ask Don Miguel Ruiz, author of "The Four Agreements," he would tell you that the world doesn't need saving. "Leave the world alone!" he states. "It doesn't need you to heal it." He believes it implies an 'I know better' attitude. Most likely, when we have the notion to save the world, we have forgotten somewhere along the line that we are supposed to be 'saving' ourselves. This statement becomes even more profound when we stop and think about the fact that we are saving ourselves from ourselves...a whole lot of saving going on!

Our concern for others distracts us from looking within to heal our own wounds. It is easier to deal with other people's pain, and that makes for a great diversion if you think about it. We have to accept that everyone we try to help has been put on our path to help amplify our own issues and need to heal. They are all displaying a component of ourselves. It takes great courage to re-instigate pain, most especially considering its source. Most of us have endured some sort of physical, mental and emotional abuse that left harsh and distorted impressions on us. Depending on our endurance or ability to take and tolerate emotional pain from our past, we will either accept its existence and allow for it to unfold, or we will keep pushing it away.

It's All Just a Pain in the Neck

Unfortunately, we are hiding all these emotions and traumas in a human body. Hidden and unresolved patterns will eventually show-up as physical conditions. Physical manifestations of emotional issues takes place when we won't, don't or can't take on emotional healing. The medical industry will now attest to emotions and stress being contributing factors in 90% of our ailments, sickness and disease. (You can find more of this information in the book, "The Healing Code.") Thankfully, when we release our emotions, much of the discomfort and disease has an opportunity to resolve itself. We see emotional healing lead to physical healing all the time, but often, practitioners will struggle with the physical cause of their client's issues until evidence reveals that it might be an underlying emotional cause.

Healing ourselves becomes even more complicated when we put our service to others before our service to ourselves. When we are distracted by giving, we can't perceive anything clearly. It creates a wide divide between what we want to do for them and what they actually need. Driven by an honorable cause, we can interrupt a person's chance to actually help themselves as well. There is no gain when we do this, and the action of enabling can actually hinder the healing process for all.

> *"Buddha tortured his body and purposely allowed himself to suffer so he could gain more understanding, enlightenment, and divinity. He felt compassion for the whole world, but not before he felt compassion for himself as a whole being. There is hope for us all!"*
>
> —KIROS

Is the glass half full because it has a crack in it?

It is important to also understand the place from which we want to give. We can't give to someone because we want to satisfy a need within ourselves. We can't help someone more than they are willing to help themselves. I have heard it said that when we do give for the wrong reasons it is like attempting to fill up a bucket with a hole in it. Our source becomes empty and the bucket never gets filled. Eventually, we deplete ourselves and cause our body discomfort, maybe even disease. It is not of the giving itself that causes this either. The real issue stems from needing to give outwardly when we should actually be giving inwardly to ourselves. This practice is like piggy backing on another's healing. We shouldn't blame ourselves when this occurs. Generosity should always be something we strive for. It just helps to know that giving for the wrong reasons or where it is not warranted will not offer the same benefit as giving from wholeness.

Emotional blockages can cause emptiness and a half-full feeling. Personal value (worthiness) is not looked at as if it were a separate entity from self-respect or self-love, but it does create a different energy. Unworthiness would also dictate a specific course of healing. If we don't feel worthy to receive, we won't accept help or perhaps even ask for it, so it is important to recognize unworthiness as a block and ask for support to clear it. Choosing our course of action and the speed we want to go is dependent on many variables. Suffice it to say, sometimes we want to move fast and other times we want to take it slow. Baby steps or long jumps, though, either way it is all a leap of faith. Sometimes out of desperation we step forward without fear, believing anything has to be better than the state we are in at that moment. We can always ask the ArchAngels for truth about what is going on, but truthfully, we have the ability to analogize with past experiences and recognize our responsibility in every scenario we find ourselves in.

Every body and mind is different and learns in different ways. What makes sense to one person will make no sense to another based on their upbringing, knowledge base and spiritual beliefs. Some of my fellow practitioners use numbers and astrology on their healing journey. Still others seek out the help of psychics. Some stay closely connected to God by prayer. Some meditate to Buddha. All of us agree, though, that love and forgiveness are the emotions we should be using to walk through all of it along the way.

"Let the Pain Pass Through You"

Letting go of blame and anger in order to love and forgive may take some time, since doing so may instigate our need to feel everything all over again. In these instances, we need to take in Prana (considered our life force) through deep breaths and then blow it out as we allow ourselves to feel the full weight of the pain without judgment or fear. It becomes easier that way. Patterns stemming from emotional blockages can be created when we resist healing. We don't want to forget or discount the past-life factor and accumulated debt from karma we collect either. If we want to recognize that as a potential cause, we would be considered prime candidates for past life regression through hypnosis.

Happiness is in the Mind of the Beholder

Being happy means different things to different people, and so our plans of pursuing happiness are as varied. We all have happy moments, and as the flow runs through us, we can feel and see the joy. If we can maintain this flow, an open and joyful heart will follow. It helps for us to talk about the happy notes of our lives, too, rather than constantly reminding ourselves of the shortcomings. We need to watch our small talk, as it is just that...small and unable to offer us a big picture, let alone a big heart. We can't perceive the weather as an up-lifter or downer either. It is always perfect. Who are we to judge anyway? Shouldn't that be the Earth's job? We need to smile at the cashier in the supermarket and at the fellow driver who cuts in front of us. Maybe they are in more of a hurry than we are at that moment.

Unhappiness brings more to itself. It is a negative energy that exists all around us and is all too 'happy' to have us join in. In the same manner, happiness is all around too, waiting for people to realize it is the better energy to be in. "Do I really want to be happy?" That is the question it all comes down to. Or maybe we should ask ourselves, "Am I having more fun being miserable?" If we look at it that way, it makes our pursuit of either more distinguishable. Happiness leads like a torch and lights the way to one's freedom. Misery, on the other hand, is a dense and very limited energy that offers confinement. I probably don't need to describe the behavior of either energy since we all have experiences sitting in both. If there is a pull to unhappiness, we will find ourselves in a space of melancholy...a sort of sadness that draws in more sadness. If we don't catch ourselves, discontent dictates every thought, word and action. "My sport team lost; My boss hates me; The economy sucks; My girlfriend did this; My husband did that...blah, blah, blah." If we listen to the space in between the words, we find the reality: "I'm a failure; I'm lonely; I'm powerless; I'm sad..." At this point, we need to understand that our past events and memories are ever present, active and triggering our present state of mind and emotions.

Our human mind won't automatically show us the big picture, where everything is coming from and why. The mind will follow an emotion, but that emotion may or may not be rooted in the present, so therefore, the intensity of that emotion, whether it be anger, resentment, anxiety, etc., may not have anything to do with what is going on at any given moment in the present. So we might think our mind is discerning what is really happening and that we are in control, but in actuality, we may be reacting. When we 'check in' with our mind instead of allowing for it to become rampant with negative thoughts, we automatically allow for our heart to engage. It is sort of like pulling the plug on the emotional drain. When we ask, "Is this reality and based on what is going on right now?" we have immediate empowerment and can assess the situation for what it is. That will help our mind to work with us and not against us, and it allows for us to bring love into the equation.

We can catch our human mind in play and take over, deciding to take a new, positive, more soulful direction. We can smile instead of grimace. We all understand how the brain works to make our face muscles move. When we are happy, we smile. When we are sad, we frown. What most don't know though, is that the brain and the face are a two way street. If we force ourselves to smile, it will register in the brain as happiness. Accordingly, when we allow ourselves to frown, we continue the sad charade.

Once we manage our behavior in a positive way, changes for the better start to flow, and we draw in better experiences. On the contrary, what we allow ourselves to listen to in our own head or from outside sources also has a profound effect on our moods and ability to stay happy. Instead of sad news on TV or radio, we can listen to happy shows and music. There is much scientific evidence to show how damaging it is to be exposed constantly to negative media. If we were to really think about it, were our bodies made to take this much negativity from outside sources in a day, week or year? We can't fake it either. The expression 'Fake it until you make it' has its place, but not here. We need to pour on the compassion for ourselves by understanding what we are being exposed to consistently. In closure, we need to make peace with ourselves and our mind and decide to allow both to be in full agreement going forward. We should want to be truthful, kind, and loving to ourselves, and do so without stepping on anyone else's life or happiness.

Love Thyself

If anyone has ever said, "You are not worthy! You are not pretty enough! You are not smart enough! You are no good!" then do yourself a favor and get a second opinion from God. There is a saying, "God doesn't make junk." We are always perfect in God's eyes. The more we make peace with ourselves about this, the more we remember that everyone else is in the same light, and that allows for an even greater flow of God's love and light to run through us. We have an unlimited potential for human/spiritual growth and abundance. I want to remind everyone, if it was to be in God's hands to wipe the sins of everyone at once, it would have been done by now. No one can realize their full potential for growth without doing the work. How could we initiate positive change in ourselves and in our future without first acknowledging who we are, what we have done, and how responsible we are for all of it?

*"We eventually become aware of our unity with the whole be-
cause it's inescapable. The awareness is wired into us, because
we're wired into the universe. We can try to pretend we're
separate from the rest of the universe, but one way or the other,
it will catch up to us and welcome us back into its embrace."*

—GAY HENDRICKS (1945–PRESENT)

"Angel of the Waters" Sculpture located in Central Park, New York

This Angelic art form has been inspiring me in various ways for
many years. I am so happy it is gracing the cover of my first book.

Part
III

In The Year 1994...

A new beginning was lingering between my curiosity about healing and my interest in the metaphysical. Both led me to become a hands-on teacher. It was around New Year's Eve when a good friend and fellow curiosity seeker and I decided to attend a psychic lecture at Borders Bookstore on Long Island. The lecture was on the varieties of energy that exist which intrigued me, but what was more appealing was the topic of physical human energy, namely; the chakra system and the way in which it can be measured. The lecturer was weird and most of the discussion didn't make sense to me, but that didn't stop me from signing up for his next class. Hesitation to do so may have been a good thing. It would have given me time to take it all in, and use my intuition to assess its value. At any juncture during our journey of discovery, we should be using our innate tools to perceive what we are allowing ourselves to be exposed to. It makes sense to sit with what we have learned and see if it resonates the next day and the day after. Did it offer clarity? Was it coming from sincerity? Okay, by now you may be getting the sense that I did none of the above.

Sometimes we can just get lucky, I suppose. Although it would be better for me to test my luck with lotto and not with my spirituality, once in a while taking a chance pays off without negative repercussion. This was one of those times. It could have gone the wrong way, but I was rescued by a healer/teacher this time. It shouldn't have to be that way for people who immerse themselves in the metaphysical world. After all, aren't they all claiming to be 'tuned in?' I've met many curious and courageous souls throughout the years that have taken too many unnecessary risks. One story in particular comes to mind of a friend who decided to meditate for three weeks all alone in the desert. At the end of all the agony, he realized that it wasn't worth the sacrifices or the time. I've personally taken plenty of risks myself, especially in the beginning of my soul searching, so I understand the zeal anyone can have for learning. It first starts with a simple energy class, then another, then another after that, and before long, luggage was packed and I was on a plane headed toward another continent! The funny thing is that we each feel and think we are doing something so incredibly good for ourselves, and who knows, in the end maybe we did. But sometimes the sacrifices and the money we are willing to spend in order to get to that place doesn't pay off. Whether it be a place of promise we are looking for, a need fulfilled, more awareness, power, knowledge, fearlessness, happiness, fulfillment, or boundless love, we need to select our paths and destinations very carefully. It is like, 'Pick a card, any card...' Each trek is full of surprises, and at some point in time, depending on our life map, we should hope to find inner truth and light.

So it was in the middle of my own internal debate over signing up for the next set of lectures that I got a call from a man named Louie who was a friend of a friend. Louie was interested in meeting me after hearing about my work, and by his own testimony, was circling around the metaphysical world since the mid-nineties. Our journeys started in similar fashion, so I recognized and understood very quickly every concern, concept and viewpoint he reiterated. Although we were trained in similar modalities, our approach to the actual work was different. We both shared the same goal, however, which was to help and assist others. We experienced similar trials and errors too, and participated in some of the same groups and seminars, all of which professed to open the doorway to ultimate awareness. His tale was an echo of mine with details of the same unskillful, naive approaches. During our conversation, I tuned in mostly to his regret of not applying some basic skills of discernment before wasting so much energy, time and money. And the discernment he was talking about was nothing more profound than common sense, logic and perception. Stuff we would be using if we could stop doubting ourselves. "I would have saved myself from a lot of trial and error, agony, and despair," Louie said. I thought he was right on target, and his phone call was perfectly timed. I thanked him for it and began to use his testimony as a catalyst to change my direction. What he said resonated, and it was exactly what I needed to hear. It remained with me throughout the years to come, as well, because, up to that point, my learning came from trial and error. That is not such a bad thing though! Eventually we wake up to truth and light.

Our Best Lessons

As humans, we learn best through inculcation (constant repetition). Most will ask if it is necessary to learn this way. The answer is no, but for some of us, it is the only way. Chances are when the need to repeat a lesson presents itself, it is because we need to gain a fresh perspective. Take forgiveness as an example. If a person can't forgive another, it may not be because they can't find it in their heart to forgive the wrong-doing or the person. The struggle may lie with the pain itself. If this is so, the only way to get us to wake up to the pain is perhaps to feel the pain again from someone else. That will take the onus off of the first person who hurt us and show us a similar scenario we created. Of course we can choose to deny that as well by staying in victim mentality, or we can decide to see ourselves as the common denominator who may have just created another situation to validate our own need for inner healing. If we can stay consciously aware of our own issues and human need to deny them, we can appropriately detach from all the drama these issues cause. Then we can face them and finally break the cycle. I personally consider every episode to be a tool we can use to chip away at physical and emotional blockages. That is what Louie's phone call did for me.

I have seen denial play out over and over again when taking metaphysical classes. I could sense the energy of weakness coming from the people in attendance, but instead of rising above it, I merged with it. There was nothing inordinate going on. Mostly it was spiritual addiction that most metaphysical seekers have. We are all vulnerable to this. For this reason and the fact that we are seekers, I believe it is advantageous for us to learn quickly through down-to-earth methods and then move on. The challenge is not just in doing the healing work, it is creating the intention to want to face what we may be in denial of. Otherwise, we stay perpetually seeking! The good news is that when we decide to 'get over ourselves,' meaning our resistance, even if it seems overwhelming at first, the more we push passed it, the easier it becomes.

A week later, I was sitting in the class given by the Border Bookstore lecturer. It was a small group, but now held in a private home, so more of us had a chance to practice what we learned the week before. The focus of this class was to concentrate on the energy of the body, the aura, and more specifically, the energy of crystals and how they feel in our hands. He spoke of the different colors of the aura, the order of the colors and where on the body they were. We practiced seeing the colors in auras on each other, and he also read each of our auricle sphere. I tried to feel the crystals, but none resonated energetically. It was clear I lacked the skills, and unfortunately, I was reminded of it by others sitting in the class. I gave it a shot, though, and attempted to do the work with an openness to learn. It was still all good, but I was thinking it would be better if I could actually see and feel what everyone else was professing to experience.

My apparent lack did make me wonder if I was the only one in class that couldn't connect. I didn't want to question anyone, so I listened and observed, testifying a few times that I tried but couldn't see or feel anything. None of it deterred me from wanting to work with the crystals though. I wanted to cleanse my own aura, so I wrote down all the instructions I needed to ensure success, specifically how the crystals were applied and what colors to use for the different parts of the body. I remember, for example, that blue should be used around the area of the neck, because that color radiates with and supports the use of the throat. But they also taught that other colors could be used too. It was all a little confusing, and since I couldn't feel anything, I started to lose my motivation.

Then came this huge book called "The Crystal Bible" which had pictures and details of every stone in existence. The more I observed and listened to everyone's happy interaction with each other, the worse I felt about the whole experience. The information became too overwhelming and confusing. My tolerance for the class faded away and so did my enthusiasm for these types of metaphysical studies. I am not sure I would even consider it more than a night of entertainment for me, since I didn't experience it energetically. It brings to mind the necessity to investigate the course, class, teacher and subjects we are attempting to involve ourselves with. More importantly, we need to question the intention behind the class and teacher as well. For instance, some people are led to learn meditation for the purposes of relaxation and peace of mind. Meditation is so wonderful for this purpose and benefits all aspects of health and wellness. Most classes and teachers offer it as a way to deal with tension, anxiety, stress reduction, clarity, focus, physical rejuvenation, enlightenment, etc. But if a meditation class is offered with the goal of exploring the realms of the psychic worlds, it creates a whole different energy and experience. Is the intention of the meditation to escape reality? To seek comfort or resolution? To gain knowledge or power? An inner calling? Whatever the intention, it needs to match yours. Approaching it with full exposure could save a lot of headaches, literally!

Who Needs Rocks When You Have Hands?

On the topic of crystals and stones, I recently observed a crystal practitioner at a wellness show. He was placing stones and crystals on people who wanted to experience the healing benefits. I was taken back by his inappropriate use. No one was cleansing the crystals in between clients. I had the need to politely state my point and then moved on. They didn't appreciate my input, but as an energy healer, I felt it was important to let them know that the crystals may take on the energies of each client. If healing each patron was their intention, what good would it be to take on another's issues? Even though some of the crystals and stones have 'self-cleaning' properties within them, not all of them do, and none of it may be reliable. The experience made me reflect on my class though, and I realized that I probably did glean from the experience.

And speaking of being back at that class, the best part of it was when it ended. Linda, who was the owner of the house the class was held in, began to prepare the room for the next session, namely, Reiki. There was something about Linda that I was drawn to. She must have felt it too, because she immediately introduced herself and welcomed us to her house and center. 'Us' included the lecturer, and he jumped in to say some very nice things about Linda. She wasn't saying much about herself, just some encouraging words about our involvement. The lecturer continued to praise her, though, remarking on what a great Reiki teacher she was. I had never heard of Reiki before, so I didn't know what he meant at first. Always excited to meet a teacher, I asked Linda what Reiki was. "It is a hands-on energy technique." When she said the word energy, she caught my attention. "What do I have to do to learn Reiki?" I asked anxiously. "Just sign up and then show up," she said with a smile. "Really?" I said. I was excited. "As a matter of fact," she added, "I'm teaching the first level next week, and there are a couple of spots open if you are interested."

"So, I don't need to be able to see energy or feel anything?" I held my posture while asking, but part of me wanted to jump up and down. "No, not really," she said. "There is no such requirement." I wanted to sign up that minute, but she must have sensed my urgency and told me to sleep on it. "Give it some thought, and if you have more questions, here's a number you can call." I grabbed the card, but just blurted out, "Can I sign up now?" I was concerned that the spots would be gone. She asked if I was sure, and I said without a doubt that I was ready to start the training. Being so impulsive is generally not a smart thing, but I felt luck was favoring me that day. Looking back, I didn't even ask any of the common sense or basic questions, like how long the training took and if there was a certificate at the end. After hearing about her and feeling her presence, I felt a sense of knowing. She was also a peaceful and mellow person. She had a way about her that could be seen and felt. I wanted that for myself and to learn all that she knew. Even though I acted on impulse, there must have been some intuition in effect, because it turned out to be one of the best classes I had ever taken. In fact, looking back on my entire journey, Reiki was and is still to date the most profound learning experience I have ever had.

Excited to Learn!

The level-one class was a two-part workshop consisting of orientation, meditation, initiation, and practice. It was a good eight full hours of class time. The first half was all intro work about the practice. Reiki is actually two Japanese words, "Rei" and "Ki," which means "universal life force energy." Universal life force energy runs through everyone, so in a sense, we all can be a Reiki healers. When anyone gets activated into the practice, it just means that they will be able to receive a little more energy than the average person. It is difficult to measure this activation at first, but in time, the work offered by a practitioner would speak for itself.

Traditionally, there are three to four levels of Reiki, but due to the ambition of modern teachers, the training and levels have expanded. Reiki is hands-on. A practitioner places their hands on and over different parts of the body, which allows energy to flow through them and then onto their client's body. There is a great story of how Reiki originated. A monk named Dr. Mikao Usui went to a mountain top to meditate and fast. After three weeks, an awareness came to him about using energy through his hands. The story of how Usui Reiki came about fascinated me, but how could it not? He discovered it on a mountain! Obvious teachings during the class included guidelines about the practice, what is allowed, the appropriate placement of our hands, comparisons of various belief systems on how to handle energy...everything anyone would need to start using the methods. There is a great book that includes so much of this work and the story behind Mikao Usui called, "The Original Reiki Handbook." I highly recommend anyone interested in becoming a Reiki to read it.

Guided to Tears

All of the class work fascinated me. I was completely immersed and excited to be able to use what I was learning. The second part of the class was a guided meditation, which was making me a little anxious. Up until that point, I had always meditated alone and not in a group. Unable to sit still and stop my monkey mind, I imagined this attempt would be no different, but Linda's explanation sounded so interesting, and I didn't want to disappoint her. I closed my eyes and went along with good intentions. Only a few minutes into it though, I kept peeking to see what the rest of the class was doing. Everyone seemed to be really focused, so I decided to get more serious, mostly because I didn't want

Linda to catch me with my eyes open. The meditation became specific as she visually guided us into a cave. It was described as very bright and filled with white quartz crystals all over the ground and walls. We were asked to stay in the cave for a few minutes to be purified and healed by the radiating energy of the color-changing crystals. Then we were asked to find a place to sit in the cave and wait for a Guide to show up and give each of us our own special and unique gift. At this point, I was envisioning myself sitting, but I was thinking, 'I'm not sure if I'm going to see a Guide. Am I really doing it? Am I really seeing this cave?' As soon as I finished asking the questions, a tall-looking person I will refer to as my Guide, stood in front of me. He or she looked like a glowing Angel and was floating around. I was fixed on the Guide's smiling face when the teacher said, "Extend your arms with open palms so that your Guide can give you your gift." I obeyed and envisioned my arms wide open, palms up. I took a step closer to get my gift.

By now I was very focused. I wanted to make sure I got to see the gift I was going to get! As I moved closer to the Guide, the Guide also came toward me. I was looking at the Guide and then down at my palms, and I didn't see anything. All I saw was a big smile on a glowing face. Once more, I took a look at my palms, and then it came! The gift arrived very unexpectedly. I was taken completely by surprise as it touched my heart and soul. I can only imagine how many blocks it removed and healed within me. To this day, I am not aware of exactly what happened. I was too overwhelmed! The meditation was still going on, but I couldn't follow. My eyes were teared, and the more thought I put into what was happening to me, the more the tears poured down my face.

It is obvious to me now that something magnificent and supernatural occurred. My breathing got labored and the quiet tears turned to audible sobbing. The images continued to linger in my mind, and I became more aware of the people around me. Embarrassed by my running nose and audible crying, I couldn't imagine that I wasn't ruining everyone else's experience. I tried to hold it back, but there was no dam I could build for those tears. Eventually, the meditation ended. Tissues were thrown my way, thankfully, because I needed them. I caught everyone watching me, but no one spoke. Many were also teared up in sympathy. Before long all of us were wiping our tears and noses. What a mess!

The teacher remained calm as she took notice of everyone, especially me. "Here, have some water," she said. "Thank you. I'm really sorry . . . ," I responded. "I don't know what happened. I never--" She stopped my apology. "No, no, it is all fine," she said, with a big soothing smile. After she handed me the water, she gave us all a five-minute bathroom break, but I stayed right where I was. Overwhelmed with thoughts and emotions that were coupled with a strange mixture of happiness and sadness, I had the sense of surrender, but not sure what I had let go of or why.

When the class convened, we went on to the next part of the workshop, which was an initiation to the actual practice. That was what I was waiting for, but after my emotional explosion the hour before, I was unsure I could handle it. Before we started, she asked us to share our experience in the guided meditation. All I could think about was being embarrassed all over again, and for two reasons; the ruckus I made, and my lack of understanding of the gift I received. I listened to how the others commented. The first person described her gift as a colorful and beautifully heart-shaped crystal that was radiating love and filled her whole presence with a feeling of infinite heartfelt joy and unconditional love. The next person saw colorful symbols and shapes floating around that changed color and faded in and out. They gave her what she described as feelings of peace, love, and joy and an inner knowing that all was going to be great for her and her family.

As I listened to each unique experience, I felt the need to start emoting all over again, and not because their descriptions were emotionally charged and breathtaking. It was because out of all of these incredible stories of interaction with gift-bearing Guides, none of them shed a single tear or even let out one tiny sound. I was the only one who took to drama! Compared to what I heard up to that point, I didn't think I had a powerful enough story to share. I tried to think and think fast about what I was going to say. Since there was only seven students in the class, my turn approached rapidly. I zoned out while trying to remember details that would make my story more interesting. 'Were there any crystals or symbols that I didn't pay attention to? What about colors? Did I see any type of colors or lights? Think! What's wrong with you anyway, crying like a baby in front of total strangers?' I couldn't keep myself from thinking how immature and stupid my behavior was.

"What did you get, Peter?" the teacher asked, but my eyes were focused on the person who just stopped talking. I had a blown-away-by-my-experience look on my face. "Peter?" she repeated. "Huh...Oh...Yes... Well...I want to apologize to everyone again, and I'm sorry if I ruined the moment." "It's OK," she reiterated. "It is fine. There is no need to apologize. These kinds of things happen all the time." 'Well, not to me!' I thought, but then opened my mouth and said, "Yes...my experience...to be honest, I didn't see that much. In the beginning, my mind wouldn't stop wandering, and I questioned everything you were saying. I was all over the place, and I couldn't follow. So I don't remember seeing anything up to that point, but after you guided us to the cave, I started to see it. The moment I started to see what you were describing, my mind went quiet."

As I became more comfortable, I went on to describe exactly what happened, and then I paused for a moment when I started to feel the tears coming all over again! "What did she give you?" Linda asked. Everyone was looking at me in suspense. "That's the thing," I said. "She didn't give me anything. After the brief hand holding, she wanted me to open my left hand, and I thought she was going to put something there. I was looking at her and then at my palm, but instead, she kissed my left hand first then the other. She gave me a big hug and a loving smile and faded away." Everyone was touched and once again, the tissues came out. Even Linda needed one stating, "Well, if my Guide came and kissed my hands, I would've cried too." We all laughed and cried in joy for a moment or two and then continued with the next person's story. And a great story it was, with amazing colors and images that were radiating a lot of love and inner knowing. She was able to recognize and understand what the signs meant for her, also a detailed description of travel beyond the cave with her Guide into space and to the stars. The class members' stories ended, but my experience will live on forever. I don't believe I will ever forget that touch or that brief moment when my Guide kissed my hands. It was truly a meditation experience I will remember and treasure always.

A 'Hands On' Experience

The time had come for the initiation. Chairs were lined up, and we were seated in a prayer position with our eyes closed. One by one, the Reiki master activated us just as her master had activated her. It was the way the Usui tradition was first taught in the Western world. We all experienced something different while getting activated. Several felt sensations; others had visions; a few had both. The mixed emotions I had of surrender and content left over from the meditation carried me through the activation. I wasn't expecting anything to happen, but my hands starting feeling strange. They began to tingle and get very hot. It felt like hundreds of needles were going through them. Then my palms and fingers became so swollen, I couldn't make a fist. I was too excited to care. We were all relishing in the knowledge that we had just become Reiki practitioners.

With our teacher's guidance, we practiced on one another, taking turns laying hands and using the time to bond. The teacher reassured us that we were all experiencing everything exactly as it was meant to be. "You all have gifts," she told us, "and Reiki helps to bring them out." She reminded us that we will each experience our gift differently, but we should all strive to help others. "Reiki is a tool for one's well being and growth, but it is also your tool to help facilitate other people's healing as well." We were told to work on ourselves every day for the next thirty days, and at least once a week to participate in the healing circle her center offered.

The next level class was scheduled three months later. Of course I was in it. I surprised myself and attended their Wednesday night guided meditation classes as well. Within a year, I managed to complete the three levels of training of the Usui and Karuna Reiki. But this was only the beginning and a subtle continuation of a journey that had started a long time before...one I had forgotten all about. A journey that eventually caught up with me when I became more willingly to merge with it.

It's All in the Monkey Mind

I was happy I got through my first group meditation, and with the added benefit of being guided. This was an avenue worth further exploration, as it gave me a sense of discovery and adventure. While in my teens, I gained knowledge of how to meditate from reading library books, but those authors always suggested to redirect thoughts that came into the head, calling them distractions. Up until taking the guided meditation class, I thought meditation was about taming the mind and keeping still. It was a way to stay quiet long enough so that peace would overcome the body. Not an easy task for anyone with a monkey mind like mine.

And what if we were to quiet it? What would we hear? I recall our writer D's story of her first attempt. Afraid to lay still out of fear she would be too anxiety ridden, she attempted it anyway on a spiritual retreat. While laying on a mat for only a few minutes, a wave of nausea came over her and she wound up running out of the room. As it turned out, it wasn't her inability to lay still and quiet the mind that made her fearful. It was what came into her mind after she cleared it! Apparently, she was blocking so much trauma from her past that when her body was exposed to even a small amount of the emotional attachment to it, she became ill. Luckily, she went on to receive trauma therapy and her life became better. After releasing the negative memories, she attempted meditation again during a yoga class. She loved it so much, she now teaches meditation to others!

At some point, after attempting meditation, we all come to a conclusion of whether it helped us or not. That determination is usually based on the initial intention going in. At my guided meditation experience during the Reiki seminar, the intention was to help us become more open to new energies. Many of us succeeded in getting into a new 'space.' Holding onto that energy space though was a different story. For a short period of time, we each experienced an expansion of the self...a sort of preview of how it feels to be without human baggage. I believe enough baggage was cleared during initiation to support the new shift in energy. Letting go of the old self is tricky for any one of us though. It is hard to resist or resolve ego issues, and this is probably the main reason why Reiki practitioners struggle early on. It would seem to mark the beginning of a transformation period. The struggle represents the ongoing process of self-healing through physical and emotional awareness.

My Reiki initiation created the need for all of us to pay attention to and clear whatever issues were surfacing. What seemed like a weekend of fun was much more than any of us had bargained for. The guided meditation played its role in assisting the process of allowance and release, although it was different for every person since we were all at different points of our own growth and awakening process. With the teacher's assistance and divine guidance, the group intention could not undermine or hasten our individual potential. Because of our teacher's motive to offer us the most benefit, I am sure we were all protected from lesser energies in the psychic realm. If not, it could have been a totally different type of experience.

To fairly assess the benefit we derive from any type of meditations, we would probably have to keep track of each intention with its subsequent outcome. After listening to other people's experiences, I found that most stayed interested for a short period of time, and only some became devoted to the practice. A few started teaching it. I'm not sure whether the method they were using or the practitioners guiding them made a difference in their ability to take to the practice. Some studied with gurus; some sought out classes, and others learned on their own. It all comes down to one question: Did it advance them on their spiritual journey? Most agree it was a great tool for spiritual growth. A few mentioned how group meditation could seem cult-like, but once removing themselves from the group, they were able to achieve better results. Many agreed that there was some sort of addiction to the energy derived from the practice, and I can see how feeling additional energy would warrant wanting to feel more and more of the same.

It is easy to see how a person can become addicted to a meditation group, teacher, and the psychic realm. It could act as a strong pull for those curious and in need to gain knowledge of everything, everyone, and mostly about themselves. There are all kinds of feel-good energies to tap into through meditation, along with an endless exploration of ideas to lose ourselves in. One way we can lose ourselves is when meditation is used to contact other sources of information and consciousness, such as; Guides, Angels, spirits, ghosts, and loved ones that have passed. Some practitioners use this as a method to prepare their students before helping them to channel, to automatic write or to do psychic readings. A well-intended teacher will instruct their students to ignore mind distractions and to bypass any temptations or urges of the ego that seek to use power and knowledge in an unhealthy way. At the very least, they would explain the consequences, which is nothing more than temporarily losing oneself. That is not always a big deal. Eventually (hopefully) we all find our way back…back to human reality…the place everyone seems to want to escape from.

Our spiritual odyssey can feel at times like a roller coaster ride. In the beginning, we are more grounded and human, but as time goes on, we learn of the many ways to escape from humanness by delving into other more profound levels of spiritual awareness. When we attempt to use them, however, we learn all too quickly that we are not supposed to use the process to lose ourselves. It is important to note that whether we go into meditation with the right intention or not, we still mingle in other realms of existence. Depending on each of our needs, abilities, and wisdom, the meditative experience will vary. Essentially, we are opening ourselves up to receiving more energy and information. This will come in the form of visuals, thoughts and messages. Gurus and enlightened human beings can handle the energy properly, but for newbies it can become overwhelming. In time, some find themselves becoming more distanced from earthly things and more interested in spirituality or in energy. Some refer to this as 'spiritual addiction.'

Usually when there is a struggle in our human experience, it is due to a long-term struggle with our own identity and lack of emotional balance. When we experience resistance, it is important to recognize the space we are in and start to review the intentions we are putting out there. There could be an energy addiction at work. Many meditation workshops and classes seem to focus on tapping into the psychic realm, believing it is the excitement people are looking for. My advice is to research before attempting anything extreme or cult-like. Even if the teacher professes to be a guru, if you're not feeling uplifted and do not feel empowered being with a teacher and/or group, then run! Meditation is a great tool when used for enlightenment and empowerment, to balance the mind, body and spirit, and to have a deeper connection to our own higher awareness and divinity. While meditating with a skilled instructor who purposely creates with you an intention of empowerment and spiritual growth, the benefit is recognized in multiple ways. Physically, mentally and emotionally, we can receive harmony and balance that allows us to have more spiritual clarity. The affect become obvious over the long-term, most especially when we look back to our state of being before we ever started the practice.

To get the most out of meditation, practice with a teacher who is dedicated to humanity in a selfless way; someone that you feel comfortable with and trust. A truly inspired teacher will be dedicated to helping their students connect to The Divine. My advice: Stay away from confusing mystical experiences! Walking around like a zombie or seeking an enlightened state for psychic thrills will put you on a path of addiction and create an emotionally unbalanced state of existence.

"When you realize how perfect everything is, you will tilt your head back and laugh at the sky."

—SIDDHARTHA GAUTAMA

The Importance of Having a Good Teacher

Growing spiritually means different things to different people. In the beginning of my quest, I wanted to maintain a feeling of oneness, especially when I started hands-on work. Practicing Reiki (whether my motivation was to help others or partially stemming from my own energy addiction issues) instigated my desire to learn more about healing. I assumed, too, that the more I learned about energy, the more energy would run through me, and this is somewhat true. Understanding energy, what it is and how it runs through our body, will help anyone's Reiki practice, but there are also emotional, karmic and astral energies to consider. We also need to understand how our client's energy can affect us physically or even merge with us, which presents the need to learn about protection, shielding and grounding, among others.

A well-informed master will teach techniques that can be applied to safeguard against issues that will negatively affect a practitioner. Hopefully they will also help clear their students of existing blockages and issues that limits their ability to be affective as healers. Energetic blockages will surface as 'opening' occurs. When a practitioner shifts their consciousness to receive more energy, the old energy patterns need to be dismissed. Some of these blockages can express themselves physically as a minor discomfort, emotionally as some sort of turmoil, or both. Hopefully all of this energy is from The Divine, but even so, to keep it coming in and appropriately used there is much to learn.

Putting aside for now the flow with The Divine, when no skills exist there is a limited flow of energy anyway. Enough external energies from clients can cause a practitioner to lose their point of reference. It is almost as if they don't know where they start and their clients end. Again, some of these energies could express themselves as aches, pains, and discomforts in the body, and they can play out as mental pictures and memories that resurface. Even though a practitioner may purposely or accidentally take on a client's negativity, she/he doesn't have to act as a dumping vessel. Preparation and awareness is key to warding off this type of merging. Without understanding of how transfer works or knowing the release techniques, the work could take its toll. Most of the body workers I have met were empaths, so this type of exchange was a major concern. Without a teacher's invaluable guidance and instruction, especially in the very beginning when merging is most likely to take place, a practitioner would find it impossible to sustain their own energy or be effective at the work.

My very first experience of energy merging took place when I was in training. I became aware of it because the sensation was very 'loud,' and by loud I mean the intensity of what I was feeling seemed amped. I wondered if the new sensation was normal, or was I just becoming aware of the subtle merges that could have been happening all along. I also wondered if others felt this, and if we as practitioners were taking on the emotional or physical issues of our clients, how long the energy would linger. As the session progressed, it took a turn for the worse. My head felt heavy, and I became depressed. My lungs started to congest, and everything in my body became achy. I started hissing with every breath I took, and seemed to have all the symptoms of a very bad cold. The person I was working on wasn't showing any symptoms, so I didn't make a logical connection about the potential for merging. I didn't know about empathy or merging at that point, so I just panicked.

I couldn't wait to call the teacher to share my concerns and in hopes of her shedding some light on what seemed unexplainable. As it turned out, she knew exactly what happened. I learned that day that I had the gift of empathy. I already knew to consciously stay out of the way and allow the flow of energy to run through my hands onto the body of the person I was working on, but apparently, when empathy is involved, precautions are necessary. Lucky for me, even without taking precautions, I woke up the next morning without symptoms. It was so beneficial to have a teacher I could share crazy notions with. That was the best part of the awakening workshops and classes. There was so much to learn in a short period of time, but with the spiritual prowess that is being uncovered, we can become lost and misguided. A weekend class is just the beginning, as a few hours of training in any healing modality barely scratches the surface. I'm sure even great conduits would acknowledge their teacher as the primary reason for coming into their gift. A great instructor will be able to help us realize what more exists within us. Without the gift being professionally uncovered, much of the self discovery would be time consuming.

My teacher's comprehension of and dedication to the healing arts were obvious to me, which helped soothe my thirst for answers. At first she offered a lot of, "Oh, don't worry, Peter. You're an empath. It's no big deal." From that day forward, I continued to have more stories to tell her and more questions to ask. When a challenge presented itself, I would call her to verify what was taking place. It took some time to distinguish between what issues, emotions and energy belonged to me versus what belonged to my clients. In the beginning when a client's issues were very intense, they expressed themselves in me as cold symptoms. The tools I applied worked most of the time and in varying degrees to release the energy that didn't belong to me. When we are new to healing and find ourselves in over our heads, some form of assistance is usually necessary to move through the confusion and concern. I always found it helpful to stay close to the teachers who offered the most help to energetically clear what I couldn't handle on my own. It is smart to do it as soon as issues arise too, before things get out of 'hand,' and that pun was definitely intentional!

Spiritual Addiction

If and when other teachers catch your attention and offer more modalities of energy work, it is a good idea to stay and master what has already been established before you move on. The title of Reiki master can drive the ego and passion, urging us to take the next step on our personal odyssey. But fascination and adventure shouldn't take us away from a trusted teacher. Consistent guidance helps to keep a new healer empowered and properly grounded. In my experience, many people that seek New Age resources are usually escaping from one thing or another and most likely themselves. Some of these resources are filling a deep need, and any one of us could lose ourselves while seeking them out. All the realms beyond the human realm are fascinating, full of information and atypical guidance. All can seem helpful, but can also be very addictive. While in search of one of these realms (psychic, astral, celestial or other) you find life becoming increasingly more difficult, you have trouble staying grounded, and you have a constant need to seek guidance from others, you have most likely become detached from the earthly human experience due to an energy addiction.

Most people with an energy addiction don't know they have one. On a recent morning I spoke to a friend (we will call her Sally) whom I hadn't heard from in a long time. We started catching up about what was new and exciting, and as she chatted, I realized how detached she sounded. I could actually feel it! As I steered the conversation I learned that she was very involved with retrieving information from Guides and Angels. Apparently it was such a huge part of her daily life that she completely detached from anything that had to do with being human. I started asking her some questions. I wanted to gain some perspective and understanding of what could be behind the desire to sacrifice one part of the self in order to elevate another. "Do you feel your body?" I asked her. "Can you feel emotion?" She responded that she could not. She had lost her balance between the human and spirit worlds. As I listened to her perspective it was clear she didn't even know how lost she was, because she felt so wonderful being in that space. Happily, I discovered that her husband had been taking care of her needs and there was nothing too deep or serious going on. I understood all too well how much joy a person could receive from being able to access The Angelic Realm. 'Who wouldn't want to stay there?' Sally was blessed to have a husband that took care of her, though. Under the influence of spiritual addiction, she couldn't remain fully functional. As in any dependency, it can create a state of havoc in daily life. Imagine not moving forward with any decision without first receiving guidance from some ethereal voice…?

Sally was a true friend, so I wanted to help her, and there was no time to be subtle. "What are you doing? Are you nuts or something?" I kept hammering questions and wasn't holding back. "Have you forgotten all the things we learned through the years about the fascination of the astral and psychic realms? Do you want to lose your husband in the process?" She was stunned at my candor. A month later, she called me back crying. Apparently her husband was considering a separation stating that he wanted a wife here on earth and not out in space. So he wasn't such an angel after all. If Sally had kept in touch with her teacher, perhaps she would have gotten the help she needed to bring her back to reality before things got so bad. Brings to mind the old adage, "Only when the student is ready does the teacher appear."

Personal History

To be an effective Reiki practitioner, a person would need to clear away any recorded history that can hinder energy flow. Since everything that we experience as a soul is remembered and recorded in our sub-conscious, it acts as a memory or energetic pattern that can become accessed. We should be seeking assistance from a teacher when looking to move beyond any recorded history, especially if part of our psyche is resistant or afraid. When we allow ourselves to be open to receive help irrespective of any discomfort we might experience, it prompts even more growth. Getting caught up in the ego would only limit our access to the many resources available. Having a great teacher by our side at the onset of our journey as a healer or just for personal expansion, would offer significant merits.

Besides using our teacher's expertise as a means to heal and a way to 'get out of our own way,' they are our information resource. There are so many aspects to energy manipulation and so many ways that it can be expressed in each of us. An experienced teacher has heard and seen enough to help us quickly understand what is going on between ourselves and our clients. Deciphering these subtleties not only saves time, it saves us anxiety. It can be very complicated and distracting at first to separate our own stuff from everyone else's. We go up, we go down, we have our breakthroughs and disappointments, but without a teacher to un-complicate things, discouragement could find its way into our practice. Simplicity is the key. When things are complicated and confusing it may be because too much effort is being put in. Even healers with many years experience struggle with this and become stuck. It is important to realize that it happens to everyone. We need to just take ourselves out of ego mode by reaching out for the help we need.

There is no need for martyrdom either, which is the No. 1 issue with most healers. We are all here to help one another, and in the process, we are continually given the opportunity to learn about ourselves, each other and the world. Some of us are sitting at the bow of the boat as navigators, some are rowing, and others sit at the stern as passengers. The bottom line: We are all heading out to sea in search of happiness, awareness and peace. Searching for the nearest port, worrying about our destination or what crazy agreement we made before we landed in the boat, will only take away from the joy of the trip. Although the big waves and occasional rough seas can make us bounce and shake, we need to stay focused on what we are learning all along the way, and that is when our teacher becomes the most helpful. Make sure whoever you choose has integrity, speaks with clarity, offers empowerment, and supports your individuality.

"Learn the craft of knowing how to open your heart and to turn on your creativity. There's a light inside of you."

—JUDITH JAMISON

Facing Challenges

From the very start, my hands felt swollen and unusually hot when doing Reiki. I was told by the Reiki master that it was a common occurrence and not to worry. "In time," she said, "you won't even notice it," and that was true. It actually became a curiosity to feel the temperature shift in my hands. One day I felt the need to bring a thermometer to the Reiki circle. I wanted to see if I could get a reading on the temperature in everyone's hands while they were working on people. It was extremely awkward for the non-Reiki's who were present, but fun for the rest of us.

Linda was open to my craziness (well maybe tolerant is a better word) and always had a smile on her face while observing our antics. She also tolerated my endless questions.

In order to gain practice and confidence, we laid hands on whoever showed up at these weekly circles. Wanting more, I was reading Reiki books and was participating in many healing circles, which offered me an opportunity to observe more closely. I also wanted to hear testimonials from both practitioners and recipients. Even with this information though, I still wasn't clear how Reiki helped heal illness. Supposedly, we are to leave it up to the universal life force energy (Reiki) and just trust that it works. Of course, I believed Reiki was healing people. I wasn't questioning that, but I was curious about the dynamics of healing in general. I wanted to know what forces were in play at the very moment healing was taking place as well as understanding the part each person played in the process. After all, there are two participants in a Reiki session: The person who is administering it and the person who is receiving it. What was the flow of energy at the actual moment of a healing? What changes taking place within a person would create a shift in their energy? If a different practitioner worked on a recipient would there be the same exact outcome for that recipient? My monkey mind wanted to know.

The practice of Reiki, especially when done in healing circles, encourages inner peace, mind silence, tranquility and calmness of the body. The flow of energy most definitely puts its participants in an altered state of feeling and being. If you can manage to keep your eyes open during one of these sessions, you can see the spaced out looks on everyone's face. Reiki energy feels wonderful, and I personally vouch to that fact. My experience has been magnificent from the very first level of training through to mastering it. It becomes even better when practicing leads to our own personal development. The self awareness it initiates prompts an easy release to our higher power. This is probably what is inferred when we hear the expression, "Let go; Let God."

During all of it though, I became distracted by my need to keep exploring. I really wanted to know how to do readings and how to see auras, how to channel, act as a conduit, intuitive, facilitator...in general, I wanted to be a better healer. My inner focus never strayed from healing and how it takes place from start to finish, which led me to support my skills with more skills. I believe I was trying to find techniques that would work better and faster, and I will admit, cooler. It would have been smarter to talk to my teacher or other fellow practitioners about my direction, but I had concerns of coming off as needy. I am aware of how I bored people to tears with all my nonsense. Allow me now to put out a sorrowful plea to all who have listened, "Thank you and I am sorry!"

"In between my discontent, my skewed attitude toward inner healing, and my inner surge to keep searching, a glimpse of support would appear. It appeared like a light gleaning from a distant lighthouse, and it would lead me back to port."

—Kiros

Inherent Gifts

I want to reiterate that we all have gifts within us! Some of these gifts are clearly active, while other gifts are dormant and just waiting for the right moment to be activated and put to good use. The time of activation is unique for everyone and varies for different reasons, but I don't believe we really deviate too far off of our original life plan. Each person claims their gifts based on their spiritual growth, meaning; these earned gifts become evident as we develop. The more development we undertake, the more of the gift appears, and what makes it really interesting is that the gifts become and are simultaneously being used as our tools to gain even more expansion. All of this guides us towards our purpose. Even with all of this support though, much can get in the way of us having a clear perspective. Having a gift is great. Being aware of such a gift or even properly using the gift is another story.

Some of the challenges that I faced early on happened while I was working on people. I would receive (ethereally) details about their condition, see images of their life events or body organs. We were told in our training not to share this type of information with clients, and for good reason. First of all, how do we know we are right? And secondly, what do you do with information like that after the fact? It was sufficient enough to be part of the facilitation of healing as a witness and conduit and not to offer random information. All of these rules were logical and worked efficiently at keeping the integrity of each session without having to put much thought in, and more importantly, to keep the doubt out.

A new client named Catherine came to see me, and as with all new people, I start the session with a Reiki orientation. I told her how the energy worked, what she may experience, how long the session would last, and that there would be no diagnosis or treatment other than the Reiki. When we were both satisfied and in agreement, I began, but not before I made sure she was comfortable with the background music, incense and lighting. After she laid down on the fresh sheet I placed on the massage table, we were all set. We both felt the flow of energy almost immediately, and after only five minutes into the treatment, she announced that the headache she had all day was fading away. The magnificence of Reiki is in the way the body responds. It receives as much energy as it needs in order to become balanced and rejuvenated. As a practitioner, there isn't much to do but stand there. Aside from creating an orderly placement of my hands on the different parts of her body, I just kept reminding myself to stay out of the way and allow the energy to do the work. We were forty-five minutes through what seemed to be an ordinary session. At the forty-sixth minute, though, things started to change.

Sometimes during a session it is possible for a practitioner to feel a few body sensations other than energy through their hands, and other times they might be able to hear tones or see images, colors and lights. We are taught not to worry about what comes up. While in the midst of an energy shift, it is appropriate to feel discomfort from whatever is being released. With Catherine, though, three quarters of the way through the session I started to hear a loud voice in my head. I knew to disregard all distractions, but this was different from anything I had ever encountered. I could literally hear someone speaking to me and also sense certain feelings that didn't have anything to do with Reiki. The voice was directed at me, but was speaking for someone else. It is these types of moments that are the most challenging. 'Do I engage with the voice, taking a leap of faith or will it be a dreadful dive?' My training didn't deal with this, and even with as many skills as I had acquired thus far, I was unequipped to understand what was going on.

My need to know was pulling me into an unknown territory. I wanted to test these boundaries. I was partially aware that my lack of training made me vulnerable to entities. Metaphorically speaking, this meant anyone who wanted to knock on the door and use my services as a channel. There is a way to take charge of this by putting a sign on the door that reads, "In" or "Not in." This offers a mindful visual to ethereal visitors. For anyone with this gift, there are boundaries we can set (or call them rules) to put us more in charge and less vulnerable, to manage how and when we want to be of service or if we want to be of service at all. With proper training, we can alleviate problems, but when we have an inner need to be validated and to gain recognition, if we have a thirst for spiritual power, or if we have energy addiction, we are much more vulnerable to entities. My choice initially was to ignore the voice which happened to be male. I continued working on Catherine, but he was relentless. It was interesting to me that he knew I could hear him, so I figured I could talk back. 'Please go away,' I said to him in my head. 'I'm not interested in what you have to say.' It didn't work.

Perhaps it was my lack of authority. I was, after all, talking to a spirit. He indicated it was of grave importance that he communicate with his daughter. I actually felt the urgency as it registered through me to her. Still, I was reluctant to be the messenger.

Through fifteen minutes of this harassment, I stood my ground. The session ended, I gave her a few minutes to adjust, and then asked her how she felt. "I loved it," she reported, and also let me know there was a moment or two when she felt a lot of emotions, but overall she said it was great. I wasn't surprised she felt something, but nonchalantly indicated that it happens to most people. In the meantime, her father wouldn't stop begging me. Although I kept saying no, I still felt his anguish. It became too much for me to handle, and I finally caved. "I don't know how to tell you this Catherine, and please don't take this the wrong way, but for the last half hour your father has been all around you. He wants to tell you something very important. I've been trying to ignore him, but he's very stubborn, and he's not letting it go. I don't know what you think about this kind of thing, but at least I'm making an effort so that he will stop driving me crazy."

I turned my attention to her father and in my mind stated to him, 'There, it is done. You happy now?' Catherine was a little surprised, but smiling. She said she was willing to hear what her father had to say. Hesitant, I waited for him to speak to me. I was breaking all the rules and hoped the message was important! I repeated the words as I heard them. "He says that he loves you very much and not to worry about the flowers." As I said the words, I couldn't believe it. 'That was all? I lost the battle with my ego for that?' Catherine started crying immediately, and that gave me even more regret for being the messenger. It took a few minutes for her to recover. My remorse prompted an apology. "I'm very, very sorry, Catherine. Please forgive me if I have upset you!" She looked at me and said, "You don't understand. I've been very upset all week about this! Last week it was the anniversary of his passing. I was supposed to meet with my mother and sister after work, and together we were going to drive to the cemetery in Queens and plant some flowers that I bought for his grave site." She went on to talk about a work delay making her late, her sister and mother left without her, which left her with no means to get there on her own. "I had trouble with my car that week, and I didn't want to risk getting stuck that far away from home." She kept sobbing through her story. "So I've been so upset and mad at myself, the car, my mother and sister...I haven't spoken to either one of them since that day, but mostly, I was upset about the flowers! This message...thank you so much for telling me!"

Staying Rooted

There was a happy ending, and it would make one think there was no harm. However it is this kind of exciting (sometimes rewarding) and fascinating experience that sucks a person in, causing them to break the rules over and over again. It was validating to know that what I heard was real, but this validation would only serve to fuel an unhealthy fire. Of course when something like this happens, we want to tell our fellow soul-searchers, and there is always one that will listen. Then that usually leads to another workshop, which won't be helpful if we attend with the wrong intentions. We all know what they say about curious cats. When we distance ourselves from our roots, meaning; our original teachings, teachers and intentions, chances are we are seeking to satisfy ego instead of learning in order to grow. That is just asking for trouble. When we look for other ways to express our gifts, we shouldn't be too hard on ourselves, but we need to always remember to keep our ego in check. Returning to our teacher for additional lessons keeps us humble. We may feel intimidated going back to them. We may have insecurities about moving forward or about limitations we want to hide, but we can't allow any of this ego stuff to get in the way of true discernment.

It is possible, too, that our not so innocent pasts might be playing a part. We can't discount the role past-lives (reincarnation) can play in our drama. It is just another way our soul expresses itself in our current lifetime that could add onto our hidden, repressed and undiscovered memories, the physical state of our body and our unresolved karmic debt.

Going Back In Order to Go Forward

In order to heal or help someone heal in the present, we may have to go back, way back. It is important to understand reincarnation and how a past life can play out in this life. The information I am sharing is based on my personal experiences and that of close friends and associates. I need to state that there is not enough pages in this book to fully explain all there is to know about this aspect of human existence, but let's start with a simple definition taken from EmergingScience.Org: Reincarnation is the religious or philosophical concept that the soul or spirit, after biological death, will begin life again in a new body. This doctrine is a central tenet of the Indian religions. Many of the greatest philosophers of the western world, such as Plato and Pythagoras, believed in reincarnation or "metempsychosis," as they called it.

Each of us have had many lives here on Earth, and depending on how we lived each one, the next should move us on to improve upon or finish what we did in the last one. Each life presents itself with a different set of circumstances, but that has no bearing on the importance of the lesson. For instance, in one life a soul can live as a king and attempt to save his country and fail. In the next life the same soul can come back as a housewife and try to do the same. This time, however, she accomplishes her goal even without having the high rank, because she spent the time in that body healing herself out of the limitations and issues all the other lives collected.

It is important to realize that whatever era we have lived in may express itself in this lifetime. I often hear of people who love a certain era and are obsessed with the clothes, the history and the art. A friend told me of several boyfriends she dated who had an extreme interest in the civil war. She finally started reading books relevant to that era and fell in love with it, which made sense since she was in love with men that were in love with it. Was it a reincarnation? That is very feasible.

In these lifetimes we are drawn to the same souls to redo, to give to, pay back or to receive. Imagine creating the synchronicity for all of this. How would it be possible, let's say, to pay back someone on the other side of the world? It is my sense that we make things easier on ourselves by sticking close to home and family, choosing to come back into situations that are familiar. Past-life experiences are within us waiting to be uncovered. It is as if they were taped on a recorder. We may not be aware of a situation being played out as a past life scenario, but most probably, we are drawn unconsciously to the different characters in them. These characters could be family members, friends, spouses, partners, siblings, bosses, teachers, lovers, and strangers (but not so strange if we consider we knew them in another lifetime). The triggers we experience are from energies of emotion that lay dormant. They are the 'finger' on the play button that starts each past life's history lesson. During these scenarios and at the right time, these triggers can be our reference point to the inner healing we need to experience.

As we experience being triggered, others are also triggered by us. If we don't release the emotion from the triggers we will keep experiencing them. Meaning, if one person annoys us and presses our buttons, the next one will too, and the next one and the next. They offer new faces with the same attributes. We will keep attracting this until we finally stop the cycle by healing from the emotion behind it. This concurrence is why most people question themselves and what they are consistently attracting. A therapist can help in this life to bring us to awareness of our attraction for the same type of person, but can they cut the ethereal ties? The cords? Can they release the energy bonds? The karma? Can they uncover a past-life pattern? There are certainly lessons to learn while in therapy, but sometimes patterns need to be broken on an ethereal level, or we will keep repeating the same story line.

> *"The purpose of life is undoubtedly to know oneself. We cannot do it unless we learn to identify ourselves with all that lives. The sum total of that life is God."*

> —MOHANDAS GANDHI

Monkey Mind vs Reiki

If you have a mind like mine, then you too have an unlimited source of energy stimulating your brain. Non-stop thoughts, ideas, questions and curiosity...an unquenchable need for answers about everything. I refer to it as 'the monkey mind,' and no offense to the monkeys, as they probably have it all figured out! It is a metaphor I use to describe a mind that allows questions and thoughts to jump from one to another without stopping. My Reiki teacher was patient with the barrage, always smiling and responding, which would create the need for more questions. She was very helpful—don't get me wrong—like all the Reiki teachers I'd encounter through the years. She had a tremendous respect for the Reiki practice and a deep compassion for people, most especially her students. Her most utilized trait while in my presence was her sense of humor. It came in handy plenty of times during awkward moments.

Heartfelt laughter is needed in our lives. It is a way our soul expresses itself, and it acts as a healing remedy for our body. It is especially useful when you get bored! I tried to discipline myself as much as I could while in sessions with clients, but I started losing interest in performing Reiki. The session treatments themselves (90 minutes) were too long. My legs would become tired from standing, my back got stiff, so I finally cut sessions down to an hour. I kept the charade going as long as I could, trying to keep a tranquil look on my face, but the monkey on my back wouldn't allow it...er, I mean the monkey in my head. At first I didn't understand what I was experiencing, but there was a frequent conversation among practitioners about resistance. For some reason, the word would come up all the time. A Reiki resistance movement must have been going on, because it became our most popular discussion.

In the beginning, the idea of healing through Reiki excited me, and I admit that being called a 'healer' fueled my ego, but the entire process became tiring. Many of the practitioners must have been doubting their practice as well, because they were making excuses every Wednesday night not to attend the Reiki circles. There were various stories about cars that broke down, chaotic days, painful body parts...all sorts of 'resistance.' Looking back, I think it was more about drama. Whatever the reasons or excuses the practitioners gave, the teacher would always say, "Whoever is meant to be here is here!" Then the circle would begin without them.

My own drama and lackluster attitude would normally necessitate a heart-to-heart conversation with my teacher, but I never pursued it. I should have. In the long run, it doesn't pay to try and sort things out by ourselves. Isolation would not yield results. Most likely all practitioners go through similar resistance issues. And let's remember that teachers were practitioners at one time. They would know what to do and how to alleviate the self-imposed 'Reiki Resistance Syndrome.' It took me awhile, but I slowly came to my own realizations. In the years that I pursued the healing arts for the sake of helping others, I was also on a journey of self discovery and self healing. It came to me that one predicated the other. So no matter how altruistic I thought I was, the entire trip had always been about me! Who knew? Is this common knowledge out there? I salute all others who reach this discovery. It obviously took me quite some time to figure out.

Was I searching to heal my karma? Probably! What about physical abuse? Most definitely! Emotional abuse? Yes, I'm sure! Some physical issues and discomforts? Why not! How about the need to rid myself of the feelings of depression, fears, sadness? Sure! And there were other issues...a long list. In the process of healing oneself, we easily tackle what we are willing to face. Whether they are minor or major, certain woes are less scary or lay on the surface and are more obvious. But start to dig deep inside the core and resistance shows up. Resistance comes in the form of a broken car that keeps us from coming to a healing circle or in discomforts, disease, drama, and of course the distractions of the monkey mind. Maybe resistance has an automatic panic switch that goes on and off when we move too fast or too slow. It is so like human nature to make it so easy to stop progress.

Going back to giving Catherine the message from her dad's spirit...was it a good thing after all? It is if we consider that she got her message, and I was reminded how much I need to work on my 'stuff.' The monkey mind will give a thousand reasons to do or not to do something. It uses whatever is necessary to get us confused and keep us stuck in our old ways. Reiki was always opening doors for me, and the monkey mind was right there blocking me from going through them.

Eckhart Tolle says, *"Being is the eternal, ever-present 'One Life' beyond the myriad forms of life that are subject to birth and death. However, Being is not only beyond but also deep within every form as its innermost invisible and indestructible essence. This means that it is accessible to you now as your own deepest self, your true nature . . . You can know it only when the mind is still, when you are present, fully and intensely in the Now."*

Am I on the Right Path?

Our paths are as unique as our hand signatures and define our pursuit of life. Intense events and certain outcomes continually redirect the path, sometimes distorting our view of it...distractions playing their part in this distortion process. Eventually, we find our way back to our original path, and what I call "our agreement." Struggles occur as we question our life purpose and/or realize that there is more to it. When we do follow our inner guide and take a few steps forward on our true path, we discover the deeper sense of our existence here and our participation in how we came to this point. In actuality, the process of finding our way helps us to find new ways and even more direction, truth and light. Our inner guide is part of a collective consciousness (a larger energy than ourselves) and can shine a light on our true path...the path that leads us to Source.

One day, I realized that my interest in mediumship was not just a curiosity; it was an awareness unfolding that had already been in motion without my understanding. At some point, my conscious self took notice, and once that happened, I was drawn further into it. This happens to all of us at one time or another on our path. We might notice a certain interest in something without fully realizing why until it feels so intense it can't be ignored. In my case, my gift of mediumship gradually made itself known, but until I was willing to accept this gift and all that comes with it, I would continue to emerge delicately.

The voices I was hearing in my head were not going away, so I thought it necessary to start developing my skills as a medium. I wanted to explore the potential uses this gift could offer in the future, and I wanted to excel at all of it. I made some inquiring calls and soon found myself the center of attention and a pawn of experimental channeling. In other words, an exploratory tool for curious souls like myself. These friends encouraged me to engage in channelling experiments, most of which I am not proud of, but at the time I thought they would advance my skills.

Looking back I realize I wasn't thinking at all. We all considered channelling to be adventurous, fun and entertaining. Sometimes inducing a 'wow' factor, but none of us took any of it too seriously or thought it was harmful enough to warrant fear of repercussion. The entire group wanted to try the experiments too, arrogantly thinking that if one can do it so can all. Once immersed, we wanted to experiment with new techniques. Sometimes we played a game of 'let's see what happens next.' We took everything we gleaned from automatic writing, channeling, psychometry, and psychic readings and explored it. We were unskilled, naive, curious, and irresponsible...all motivated by each other's curiosity, ego and underlying motives. It was surprising that we didn't get into trouble. No one became possessed or anything, but none of us got anywhere on our spiritual journey either.

I stayed with the group for a while then backed away when what I was channelling became more accurate and detailed. Not that I didn't have fun at first, but when people started asking really heavy questions with serious concerns about their lives, I felt uncomfortable. Dealing with their issues caused me undo pressure, and I didn't want to be their channel of bad news. Up until that point, the information we were receiving was general and basic, offering opinion about everything from the earth and climate change, to energy healing and psychic awareness. Some personal solutions did find their way in, but no actual tools we could all use for more self-empowerment or self-growth, and that was what I was really interested in.

Downloading

When I look back at my first channelling experience (the night I was desperately trying to finish a calligraphy homework assignment and the Angels helped me draw), I realize I was young, innocent, and very sleepy. The ability to channel came 'automatically,' hence the term 'automatic writing.' Regretfully, I pushed the memory of it away after being reprimanded, but that didn't keep the skill from coming back. My first realization of it was during the guided meditation at the Reiki initiation and then again during the Reiki session with my client Catherine. Obviously much preparation had to take place up to this point for the gift to come through, although I wasn't knowingly aware of any of it. How could I know what I didn't remember? But that is the point; I didn't have to. There was a part of me that was already seeing and guiding my direction. Hmmm, perhaps this was the focus of my early childhood lessons with the Asian teacher?

There were times in meditation when I was just sitting comfortably in a chair and breathing normally, getting into what I called 'a good space.' When I felt this peaceful and balanced state, I would think of a question and actually hear an answer. It seemed to come natural. I'm sure now, looking back, that information from my Guides and spiritual teachers were always trying to come through, but my monkey mind was hard at work keeping me from hearing their remarks. Back then balance meant something different to me than it does now. If my body didn't hurt in any way or cause any symptom that would distract me, I deemed it balanced. If my mind wasn't distracted by negative thoughts, it was in balance. I didn't realize that all sensations of the body and all thoughts can give clues that lead to healing. I didn't know that all the pictures, images and thoughts I was trying to repress were all trying to tell me a story or direction I needed to hear. This realization came later.

Before I understood that I was channelling, not much made sense, and if I would have sought out a teacher, (s)he might have been able to help me decipher the difference between my intellect and their wisdom. Self-analyzing helped to eliminate some clutter, though, and it also helped me discard unclear, misguided monkey nonsense. The biggest discovery was how much of the good stuff I was wasn't hearing because I was listening to the not-so-good stuff. Having a stenographer would have been helpful, too, since I was forgetting as much as I was remembering! Writing everything down wasn't always feasible since I was channelling with my eyes closed. A recorder might have been useful, but I don't like hearing my own voice. And I am not sure it would have helped in every instance anyway. There were times in group channeling meetings when I was channeling for about half hour and no one's recorder was able to pick any of it up. No one could figure out a mechanical reason why either.

Practice makes perfect, and after years of meditating, I got better at holding 'the space.' In time, I was able to open my eyes, write quickly and go back into it. I would take my interpretations and words and seek out a type of translation that would make sense. Sometimes, words would come in one by one. They wouldn't make sense at all until I read all of them consecutively and realized it was a sentence. I guess they (those behind the voices) didn't have faith in my ability to download the whole message at once! Not that being able to read a whole sentence guaranteed I understood what I was hearing or that it answered the questions I was asking. I often thought it would been nice if more of the information they were offering was about me. Answers to personal questions I had about my life and journey would have been helpful.

They way they were communicating was always different. Sometimes it came in as a knowingness. It was info that felt too real not to be true. There were visual observations, shapes and images, and besides being able to see them, I would hear words and people talking to me. These are all known as psychic gifts, but rather than giving you my interpretation of them, here is a list from wikipedia.com:

Clairsentience (feeling/touching)
In the field of parapsychology, clairsentience is a form of extra-sensory perception wherein a person acquires psychic knowledge primarily by feeling. The word "clair" is French for "clear," and "sentience" is derived from the Latin sentire, "to feel." Psychometry is related to clairsentience. The word stems from psyche and metric, which means "soul-measuring."

Clariaudience (hearing/listening)

In the field of parapsychology, clairaudience is a form of extra-sensory perception wherein a person acquires information by paranormal auditory means. It is often considered to be a form of clairvoyance. Clairaudience is essentially the ability to hear in a paranormal manner as opposed to paranormal seeing (clairvoyance) and feeling (clairsentience).

Clairalience (smelling)

Also known as clairescence, it is in the field of parapsychology, clairalience is a form of extra-sensory perception wherein a person accesses psychic knowledge through the physical sense of smell.

Claircognizance (knowing)

In the field of parapsychology, claircognizance is a form of extra-sensory perception wherein a person acquires psychic knowledge primarily by means of intrinsic knowledge. It is the ability to know something without a physical explanation why you know it, like the concept of mediums and mediumship.

Clairgustance (tasting)

In the field of parapsychology, clairgustance is defined as a form of extra-sensory perception that allegedly allows one to taste a substance without putting anything in one's mouth. It is claimed that those who possess this ability are able to perceive the essence of a substance from the spiritual or ethereal realms through taste.

My Message

Once, while trying to write a brochure that could encapsulate what I do, I asked my Guides for verbiage. This is what I heard: "You are a clairvoyant, clairaudient channel that allows your Angel Guides to come forth and accommodate healing. As a gifted empath with extraordinary sensitive sensor-like ability, you can pinpoint existing and/or forming energy blockages that cause aches, pain, and discomfort in the physical and subtle bodies, aura, chakras and energetic field." After channelling this response, I added, "My personal belief is that all illnesses are related to energy misalignment in the subtle bodies, and since the physical is the effect of the subtle bodies, so are the illnesses. With the guidance of God and my Angel Guides, I will channel specifically what is needed and appropriate for each individual at their present state of consciousness, growth, and experience. What creates the healing is in the moment-by-moment relationship between the recipient and the life force. At a healing session, the life force will make as many adjustments one allows and trusts it to make." This channeling experience acted as a glimpse and insight to what was unfolding in my life, helping me to see what direction my healing abilities were going to take.

Staying in 'The Space.'

I'm sure all of the meditation work I did on my own acted as self-training for channelling. It helped make it easier for me to be in a receptive space. We all have to start from somewhere, and for me it was yoga, Reiki and meditation that prepared me for channeling. Although my childhood experiences with the Angels and my Asian teacher would prove I always had the abilities even though they seemed to disappear for a while. I truly believe that life took hold of me as it does to everyone, bringing out the ego and the monkey mind. My friends had frequently talked of their struggle with staying still in their bodies and mind while meditating, and of course I understood. Even the slightest noises would bring me out of the space, most especially in group meditations. When there was an occasional hmm or an audible deep breath taken by someone, I wanted to know who it was, and if they were just showing off or possibly just expressing boredom. Curiosity always got the best of me. Still, in many ways, group sessions have proven beneficial to me, and I promote them to others for their potential to tame the monkey mind while increasing energy, advancing personal growth, and raising awareness.

Automatic Writing

In the same holding space of meditation, channeling, and inspiration, I would occasionally write poetry. Nothing fancy...just a few sentences that related to me at the time. In one such moment I wrote this acknowledgment and tribute to my life, nature and the endless support that I have been receiving on my journey here:

Walking along the path of joy,
Looking in awe at what life has created for me to enjoy.
In every step of the way,
I see myself reflecting back,
And every beat of my heart,
Gives in return its tribute to life.

An Astral Being: Friend or Foe

It was suggested by my fellow channelers that we should all attend a lecture of real, top-notch pros. It was meant to give us all a chance to get some more in-depth answers for our questions, but all it did was open up a psychic door to more nonsense. Still, some group members were drawn to nonsense. It took a few more years for everyone to realize that there were harmful consequences to being exposed to erroneous information and belief systems, astral entities, and the like. In time, it became clear to most of us that some teacher's had the need to control us through fear. Their intentions weren't apparent in the beginning. We were most likely blinded by our various degrees of fascination, but danger became apparent as anxiety and crises presented itself in each of our lives.

Basically, the work was instigating group members' cycles of emotional drama without offering resolution. It seemed too that this instigation was intentionally being done to keep everyone stuck and intimidated. There was a sort of brainwashing going on as we were given instructions for energy techniques recommended by astral entities, which went on to cause some people mental, emotional, physical, and spiritual imbalances. As the imbalances arose, there was no awareness of their origin, so no one was really trying to reconcile them. There was much disorientation and a constant dependency on the entities for solutions to these ongoing cycles. Of course the so-called solutions were nonsense, which made everyone even more vulnerable and controlled. It would seem crazy that anyone, especially someone who can sense and feel negativity, would allow for this kind of abuse. Being a channeler and coming from this perspective, I can admit that it feels good and very fulfilling to be useful by providing this type of information. Let's partially blame it on karma, too, for everyone involved. As for the astral entities hard at work behind the scene, they are playing the role of a guiding force, offering advice, instructions, solutions, and a helping hand. At first, it is not easy to recognize this as anything that is negative. Since they know things about us, though, they can manipulate energies, create visions and thoughts, plant ideas and stir people's emotions. They can hide their real intentions from us humans with ease.

Many people ask me why astral beings would be doing things like this to us. I could think of many different reasons. First, I believe they become attached to someone and use them as a source of energy because they are in spirit form and want somehow to access this physical reality. Our energy can be assessed through our aura, and they look for weaknesses, limitations, secrets, inner thoughts, our fears, desires...all our vulnerabilities and unfortunately, what is most sacred to us. They use it as a doorway to access our emotions and then amplify them with more negativity; such as loss, uncertainty, despair, emptiness, etc. Once a person is vulnerable, they start looking for a quick solution so they can create a bond. At that point, the person is very easy to manipulate, especially if they have no idea what is going on.

To really cement the bond, they can add sexual energy, making people 'feel so right' about who they are attracted to. This energy can make the manipulated person believe they are with the right people, in the right place, at the right time. It sometimes takes quite a while for all of this astral foolery (scam) to be exposed. Although it shouldn't take years, it unfortunately did in my case. The astral beings make us think they hold the answers to all we are searching for. So it makes sense that we shouldn't be blindly listening to anyone who is giving us information from the psychic realm considering how any one of us can be caught in an astral being's web of confusion. Unfortunately, this is not an over dramatization. If any one is a little curious about their life and seek out a psychic reading, as long as they don't take every aspect of it completely serious, there is usually no real harm. But some people actually will surrender their power and parts of their life. I have seen people sell their homes and move away because of 'advice' they received. Others lived in constant fear and limitation, and still others altered their belief systems, religious affiliation...too many manipulation stories to list. And the degree in which they relied on these entities was over the top as well, some not able to make a single decision without channelling advice.

There was one such lady who was so devoted she practiced non-stop, believing every exercise she was given would be able to increase her flow of energy. One day in Q&A, she showed us the blisters in her arms from this over-practicing. Unfortunately, instead of someone advising her to seek medical attention, the teacher praised her dedication to the work, and we all sat and listened intently so we could learn more. A year later she wound up in the hospital with heart issues. A series of tests later, they found several tumors in various parts of her body. Within a few months, she passed away. In fact, two to three people a year would pass away in that group, and some had deaths within their families as well. To think that most were there to lengthen their lives and achieve well being...

Light Workers

There are plenty of channels and teachers out there that do wonderful work and focus on empowering people. They utilize their gifts to offer solutions and act as liaisons, helping their clients without claiming to know it all. Simply stated, they act as a tool and vehicle of assistance to bring awareness and inner wisdom to those they work with. These heart-centered healers and teachers are wise, loving, wonderful, authentic, and enlightened human beings. They channel highly evolved beings and rescue all the poor souls like myself from manipulation by unscrupulous entities and beings. I thank God and my Angels for them. I speak from experience, and I am most grateful for every person who came into my life at the exact time I really needed them.

The Common Goals

Finally, there is a bonding that takes place within a group. I'm not only referring to the typical bonding of people with common interests. While deep in the throws of self exploration, we expose ourselves and start to feel close to all or some of the group members. It might feel good at first, but as we move in growth, so does our interests, and one day we realize we are not at the same point of focus anymore. It is possible that we can feel and sense this transformation in others. When differences in ideologies and growth start separating us from the group and teachers, it is obviously time to leave, and that is when we get a fresh look of what we learned. In the process of evaluating and unraveling, we can decide what we will hold onto and what we will release.

Sometimes a break up from the group can fill us with doubt about ourselves. 'Did I mess myself up in some way? Who will I call to fix me now? Is there a lesson in this? What did I learn? Why didn't I see this sooner?' All these questions are normal and can be used to identify the positive and the not-so-positive outcomes in the experience. When committed to a group for the purpose of learning and growth, it is important for everyone to have common goals, but when those goals are attached to the betterment of others, it would make sense that our well being is at risk. It could render us powerless and is the perfect scenario, by the way, for spiritual attack and all the other nonsense to occur. When there are honorable causes for humanity, and there are some out there, we won't sense a loss of the self. An authentic group that is driven by goodness, has the right motive, and is empowered by God would help us find ourselves, not lose ourselves.

As I look back, I don't have a clue what the goals were for the group of channelers. It was very obvious to decipher the individual goals of group members though. Their thirst for knowledge, power, recognition, and their huge egos were apparent. There was also a need for survival, since most were preparing for doomsday. During lectures some of these people would ask fear-based questions. They were confused and limited, often in competition with one another. All this negativity that each of us could have used to create change in our lives. Add the release of karma and all that comes with it, and here comes the growth and awakening. Amen!

Teacher's Pet

Within the group there were an elite few that were held in higher regard by the teacher and encouraged more than the rest of us. Everyone was vying for those few spots too. They were often given titles, put in charge of events, and were constantly being recognized for their advancements. According to the teacher, they had specialties to share with the world that the rest of us didn't. None of this resonated with me. At first I thought it might have been a jealousy issue, or perhaps they were better practitioners than I was. It was true that some were better channels, healers and readers, but eventually I realized their 'specialties' were really their physical attributes. The prettier the woman, the faster they advanced in class. There were plenty of stories and gossip about who was sleeping with who and other such nonsense. There is a lot of sexual exploitation in the New Age arena.

A quote by Jesus found in the New Testament taken from the Gospel according to John: *"You shall know the truth, and the truth shall make you free."*

When Entities are Stuck

In general I find that people love channeling and physic readings. Having personal sessions can be very exciting, informative, and entertaining, which is why many visit lectures and workshops to find talented channels. When channeling is taken seriously though, it can be harmful. Some people are willing to completely surrender to what is being told to them, totally disregarding their own intellect, intuition and logic. It is difficult to figure out what a channeler's intention is, or if they are working with cunning spirits as their guides. We need to consider that when we were in spirit, we made a choice to come here to grow in awareness and uplift further and closer to God. Astral entities, on the other hand, may be stuck in the astral. Even if they seem to be knowledgeable, we may not know what they are connected to. We may be struggling down here and trying to figure out who we are or where we are going, but that doesn't mean an astral being is further on their spiritual journey towards God and awareness just because they are in spirit.

Entities stay around us, earthbound, out of fear of going to the light. They had lives just like the rest of us, having their own personality, likes, dislikes, families, and friends. They attach themselves to living souls, because they don't have their own physical body. They don't necessarily choose someone like themselves. As long as a body is alive, it is a host candidate. At the time of death, an entity did not go to the light, nor did they want to take the path of awareness. Most likely, they didn't want to let go. They choose to cling on to life, possibly out of fear of what we would consider God's judgment; like sins, guilt, punishment, etc. Some stay back because they desperately want to give an important message to a loved one, and others because they don't know or realize they're dead.

When an entity attaches itself, it brings along its traits, hobbies, conflicts, beliefs, fears...everything that made up its human existence here on Earth. They have many different ways of expressing themselves in their host. An inhabited person might feel as if they were all of a sudden a different person. Their attitude might change and they might act in ways unlike their normal selves. Sometimes an entity would choose like minded souls, meaning if they liked to drink they would choose an alcoholic. Does that mean people who drink frequently have entities attached to them? Not that I have done a study on it, but I have noticed many people who drink do have entities attached to them. Perhaps being intoxicated makes them an easy target, or maybe they drink because they are so uncomfortable with inner conflict from an entity. What came first, the chicken or...? One thing is for sure: An entity attachment by definition represents and supports the concept of limitation, both the human's incapacity to defend themselves and the entities' physical restrictions.

Although some entities seem to offer good advice or healing skills, we need to consider their choices after leaving here. If they didn't go to the light, that would suggest they are not light workers! When we meditate and open ourselves up to the light by expanding and opening our aura, it is so we can receive guidance. That makes us a potential host in the making. Think of aura as a shield. Now picture the Star Trek Enterprise and remember when the ship's shield was down, the crew would get tense, and everyone hustled to man their stations. The captain would immediately call the engine room, "Scottie, give me an evaluation of potential damage and repairs." Missiles become deployed, but a second before impact, the shield goes back on. Thanks to Scottie, another job well done!

Gaps or openings in an aura makes it easy for an entity to attach itself. When the aura is strong and vibrant and full of light with an expanded aura, entities are attracted, but it is much harder for them to penetrate. Keeping our aura closed off will send a visual message to nearby entities that our body is off limits. The more we practice closing techniques, the better we become at it. It will also help us recognize when we need to close it as well. Eventually, we can just command it by saying, "Aura close down."

> *"It really boils down to this: that all life is interrelated. We are all caught in an inescapable network of mutuality, tied to a single garment of destiny. Whatever affects one directly affects all indirectly."*

> —MARTIN LUTHER KING, JR.

Hypnosis and Past-Life Regression

Hypnosis is a state of being that allows the conscious mind to be bypassed by suggestion and selective thinking. The conscious mind is the part of us that rationalizes, reasons, and passes judgment. When we dispense with the need to pass judgment and rational thinking becomes suspended, it can be said that we are in hypnosis. I have only great things to say about hypnosis, and that comes from my personal experiences being hypnotized and as a hypnotist. My first experience happened in 1996. Although I'd use self-hypnosis tapes up to that point, it was my first in-person session with an actual professional hypnotist. Not only was I going to be hypnotized during this first session, I was attempting to be led through a past-life regression. I was skeptical at first that I could be put under, and I didn't feel comfortable for some reason looking into my past lives. Perhaps it was resistance, but I try never to allow resistance to stop me. In fact, that usually makes me more interested!

Going through the process of past-life regression was intense and different from anything I had ever experienced. It was somewhat the same as my guided meditation experience and much more exciting than listening to the self-hypnosis tapes; not that they weren't helpful tools and awesome for the mind and body. The personal session was more spontaneous, had more flavor and it was a lot more interesting. It was like going to the movie theatre and watching a movie about myself that I wrote and directed a thousand years ago. Even better, instead of watching it on a little TV, it was huge on a big screen in 3D. I have heard other stories about my life through readings, but that was like trying to see through a tiny crystal ball compared to this.

What I experienced was fascinating and unexpected, and that's the most awesome part of hypnosis. There is no way of knowing what is going to come up. It is all a surprise. Was I a beggar, a king, a killer, a princess, a soldier...a nun? During the session, I could see different scenes of my life being played out. At first, it seems like a distant but strangely familiar story that was somewhat relating to my present life. This is much like all regression experiences and how they start out. As it progresses, the characters and their roles and participation in our lives become much clearer, offering us a glimpse of what we need to work on and to let go of. All the information retrieved from our past-life story helps to bring transparency and understanding, not only regarding our present situation, but also the possible causes of behaviors from ourselves and others.

If could be a scenario of some sort of drama, conflict, misunderstanding, struggle, murder, etc. No matter what we see, though, it should help put everything into a new perspective that offers understanding of feelings and reactions that relate to our relationships. Steering away from the drama and seeking closure should be the main focus of all this transparency. Since all of the past stuff expresses itself in the here and now in the form of emotional, mental, or physical turmoil, just knowing about it (and the karma attached) will bring more clarity and under-standing, maybe even unconditional love when it involves people we are close to.

Down With The Drama

It is important to acknowledge that our energy to attract repeat scenarios can be amplified once an original trigger is awakened but not healed. Also, amplification can occur if we don't recognize it as our responsibility to heal and instead lay blame on another. I really believe this could explain why the rate of divorce for a second time marriage is even higher than the first. Many people leave one partner and then go into a similar situation without healing from the first or learning their lesson. I can think of a few different ways and approach-es that can resolve such a cycle. First thing I would do is look into the history. Is there a past life issue? If so, then clearing the past life will definitely terminate or at least minimize the lesson. I would then at-tempt to cut any energetic bond between the two people (possibly a life lesson cord), which should result in a peaceful closure if the rela-tionship ended badly. But even if it is an ongoing relationship, cutting the bond will bring more balance and a healthier, more empowered interaction. Healing the repeating patterns always jumpstarts spiritual growth and awareness.

If none of the healing occurs, there is the potential for pieces of their puzzle to go missing or unnoticed. There is what I call 'energetic bundles' all around us that give us the exact ingredients and perfect recipe for our growth and evolution here on Earth. These bundles could also be called 'people.' Energetically we play specific roles in one another's lives. It's not just physical chemistry at work. We are drawn together because of this ac-commodating energy. Even if we don't actually believe in the concept of reincarnation, energies still get exchanged. As we grow and learn and tol-erate more from one another in the spirit of awareness, karma gets paid off anyway. No one gets left behind and everyone wins. This is a divine plan since everyone is living in a different state of growth and awareness. It should be said, that no matter where we are on this journey, we are exactly where we are supposed to be!

For any of us that are questioning other people's intentions towards us or our own for that matter, consider the drama. Where could it be stemming from? Are we trying to resolve our own lessons with someone? Perhaps a new understanding of these energetic ties will help to better understand why there is difficulty in breaking away from repetitive situations. Choosing to distance ourselves from drama is good, but distancing ourselves from the people we are stuck in that drama with may not be enough. If there remains a sense of unfinished business between two people, it will create ongoing chaos that will be expressed in all sorts of pain and suffering. No matter whether we leave this person or not, the energy we share with them could stay and be attached to the next person. Permanently cutting the energetic bond would speed up the letting-go process and free each from many negative feelings and reactions. I want to repeat this important message. Once the energetic ties are cut, the same person can't energetically bond with you in that way ever again...in this lifetime anyway. That is not to say that you might not accidentally bond with them, but as long as you eventually become aware of what you are doing to stay connected to that person, you can release the bond again.

What to Expect

Although all sessions are customized, for the most part regression work is similar for everyone. We set an intention that is agreed upon at the beginning of the session. It could be something like, "We intend to use the information we obtain toward improvement of life." If the client has a point of focus established, whether it be a difficulty with another, headache or whatever, the practitioner will include any and all in the joint intention, making it the most impactful for growth. From there the hypnotist's job is to help get the client into a space of trust and comfort so they can let go of their conscious and reach the subconscious. I usually begin by helping my client relax their body, bringing them into the moment and releasing any tension from their day. I do this with a color visualization technique. Once they are mentally focused on the colors, I tell them to contract and then release muscles as directed by their own stress, aches and twinges. I ask them to stretch the parts that need it and to take in deep breaths to assist. Eventually the body will relax, and when it does it is time to address the mind where all the concerns are stored. Together we guide the release of these concerns with a form of 'letting go' meditation. This technique allows the awareness of both the conscious and subconscious to surface and then participate in agreement with one another. The clients contribution of their conscious and subconscious selves is the most important part by the way. It is necessary to help bring them to the point of letting go. With this in place, everything is in alignment, and we are ready for a great session to commence. At that point, too, I am ready to be their guide and to offer intuitive support and insight.

All practitioners should make their clients feel encouraged and offer assistance from start to finish. If they don't feel comfortable and safe while going through each step of hypnosis, they won't achieve a deep hypnosis and get into the 'space.' Remember too, that what comes through in hypnosis is potentially something a person has been running from or incapable of seeing on their own. A practitioner is helping the client "boldly go where no man has gone before." (Back to Star Trek!) When trying to achieve our own healing, we need to be able to see clearly what needs to change. Through hypnosis we can see and hear what we need, but it can seem scary to the conscious mind. This is why it is so crucial for a practitioner to make their client feel comfortable and supported as well as making sure their conscious and subconscious minds are in agreement with what is about to transpire.

Once my client reaches that depth of safety in the session, the rest of it falls into place. I always have a flexible approach, recognizing when adjustments need to be made or energy redirected. Usually, the story the client is viewing under hypnosis is in sync with their readiness to release the emotions that are attached to it. When they are welcoming the healing, I can help them find the closure. Energetic blocks get removed when the subconscious mind is in control. Which leads me to an important point: The job of the practitioner is to assist and co-create with the client, not to predetermine the outcome. I always follow the flow and help them release the emotions and energies that support their process. The client's healing and recovery is quicker and easier this way. At the same time, by keeping this vantage point, I receive the most satisfaction and joy from my participation.

Karmic Partners

Once in session, the most profound issues will start to surface. Most often I would hear of relationship challenges. The person with whom we have the most intense and frequent conflict with in this lifetime is most likely the one we had the same or worse conflict with in a previous life. Remember cause and effect: Whatever happens to us in any lifetime is registered in the soul. So even though we don't remember what took place in a previous life, the energy between our souls will linger, making us either feel uncomfortable around a person or drawn to them, or both. This person could be a family member, friend, lover, spouse, coworker, or stranger. The closer the relationship to us, though, the more chance we have of resolving a past life history (karma) together, not that we can't have a resolution with a total stranger either. Without a memory of it, issues could take quite some time to unravel. After all, how many of us are aware enough to blame our current difficulties on a past-life experience? It might take endless effort (which is why we keep repeating drama), sacrifice, courage, and compromise to work out such relationships. (I am smiling as I say this, but some call this marriage.) Take into account, that the more times our souls have experienced the same karma, the more buildup of drama and emotional scars will be attached to it. It becomes almost impossible for us to see clear through this much suffering and emotion. Stirred up emotions create a muddy perception. There is the other side of the coin, however, where we can have a peaceful and benevolent relationship with someone because of our past life with them. Some of us learn sooner than later.

Let's say for instance that we took someone's life during one of our lifetimes. We might spend the rest of this life trying to repay them through self-sacrifice, loyalty, friendship, parenting, marriage, etc. Hopefully, when we were in spirit, we planned our lifetime here accordingly. Maybe we signed up to become their parent or sibling, lover or caretaker, and we are willing to release the karma by repaying the debt to them. Whether it is in this lifetime or another, I believe all debt gets paid, so there is no rush. Many people get a little discouraged about karma, past lives and debt payment, and I can understand their frustration. As a practitioner who immerses oneself in other people's karma on a daily basis, I can say there is a lot of frustration that can be avoided. We need to realize that not everything can be figured out. All we can do is try our best to live a good life and clear as much as we can. In fact, most of you are probably making your own closures now just by reading this book! Without even thinking about karma, you are doing a fantastic job of helping yourself grow and learn. How awesome is life!

Hypnosis is not the only tool or preferred method to release karmic debt, but for anyone who truly wants to seek out an inordinate way of releasing emotion, it is a great way to go. It doesn't always have to be so deep, either. First time curiosity seekers can do a more mellow session to start, building up to a past life regression after feeling comfortable about the process and their practitioner. It can be categorized more simply as a tool for self-exploration, discovery, insight, and resolution. Sessions I perform also focus on clearing energetic blockages put on the soul through the subconscious. I find that to be the most effective way to stop negative emotional patterns. Energy blockages from past-life experiences can create impressions deep within. The saying goes "as above, so below." These blockages can, in effect, mold our character and contribute to our patterns and cycles.

Stand in the Sun and Grow!

Earth, among other things, is the place we come to live, learn, create, and resolve. For those of you that are trying to figure things out...tolerating themselves and others in the process...enough helpful hints have been given throughout this book to help you start. My hope was to give you a different perspective. The stories of my learning process were purposely sewn into the fabric of this book to show my own humanness, frailties and need for growth. Together we can be inspired to live fully and consciously and to help each other discover how to gain full power while we are here from all the tools and teachers we have to gain from. A quote found in the "Sacred Path Cards" by Jamie Sams, a Native American writer and orator, states, *"In Native American culture, we see everything as being alive. Each living thing has a specific role as a teacher and family member. Everything on Earth, whether stone, tree, creature, cloud, sun, moon, or human being is one of our relatives. They represent the sacred living extensions of the Great mystery, placed here to help humankind evolve spiritually."*

Intuitive Healing

"In·tu·i·tion, int(y)o͞o'iSHən. Noun meaning: 1. The ability to understand something immediately, without the need for conscious reasoning. "We shall allow our intuition to guide us." 2. A thing that one knows or considers likely from instinctive feeling rather than conscious reasoning. Synonyms: hunch, feeling (in one's bones), inkling, (sneaking) suspicion, idea, sense, notion."

That is Webster's definition, and here is mine: Intuition is our ability to receive input and ideas without knowing exactly how, where or from whom we received them. You simply know, though, it is not coming from just your human self. Like creativity, intuitive inspiration often occurs when we immerse ourselves in an activity that brings us joy and fulfillment. I believe it makes itself known in many forms.

Although I didn't understand the meaning at the time, the name "Intuitive healer" was given to me because of how I moved my hands involuntarily during a session. When I first started directing my energy to heal others, I understood where messages and energy were coming from. Consciously, I had no control over any of it. I have confessed to ego tendencies, but never took credit for any healing energy that came through me. My belief was that it was coming from God. I felt an inner connection to God while receiving the energy as well, and I wanted—almost expected—the guidance and direction for each step I needed to take to come in to me. I can't imagine it came from my own intellect. Early on, though, I was looking for validation that I was being used as a conduit. Perhaps that is all part of the process of growth and how God works through us. God helps us overcome the doubts by giving us validation here and there. We are God's children, after all, and every child needs to know they are okay and doing well. God knows what we need, even when we don't. For me, trusting that the energy was coming from a divine source let me release any doubts about what part I played in someone's healing process. It allowed a free flow of energy to move through me and onto the people who were willing to receive it. My intuition helped me distinguish their level of awareness, too, and I used it as a tool to help them move along on their journey.

I was lucky enough to have both clients and friends willing to let me work on them. My hand-moving style began to tone down through practice. I was happy about the new way of applying energy, but I wasn't sure my client's were getting the full mojo without all the hand gesturing.

Call it a control issue, but I needed to be assured each client was receiving the full benefit from my services. The energy did come through though, so I had to own it. I was learning about myself during all this too. While working on other people's issues, I was able to see my own limitations, which led me to trust in the process, honor myself and then finally to let it all go. Honestly, if it wasn't for God's helping hand and guidance, there wouldn't be much worth writing about.

> *"What comes through intuitively blends with us and becomes part of us, stirring up excitement as we begin to 'own it.'"*

> —KIROS

"Let me see...now how can I explain this?"

The hardest part about intuition is explaining it! Even though I was beginning to understand the method I was using, I had nothing structured I could define or demonstrate. It shouldn't be necessary to dissect the tools we use, but in order to explain it to inquisitive clients, to teach others, or to improve my own affectedness, I needed to know more. The very first couple of times my hands were being guided intuitively, it was obvious and awkward for myself and the client. Once, as I was just about to place my hands on top of a woman's head, they shook uncontrollably. I attempted to start over a few times placing my hands over her shoulders, knees, and other places, but nothing helped to stop the shaking. I was aware that it wasn't due to my lack of control or discipline. Instead, I had a sense of an ethereal energy surge merging with my own human energy. This new energy wasn't taking me into an alternate state of thinking, but the shift made it difficult for me to control the session.

Days later, a session took the same turn. My hands started shaking and funny enough, it looked like I wanted to strangle her. So I pulled back, took a couple of deep breaths, and tried again to engage, but my hands shook even more with every attempt. Not having a clue of what was going on, I canceled the session, claiming 'Reiki malfunction.' I politely explained my predicament, apologized and offered extra free time for our next appointment. Even though I had some success at controlling it with other clients, for some reason, I wasn't confident it would go in that direction with her. It was only fair that I offer an explanation and not use her as a guinea pig.

To my surprise, the strange and peculiar hand-motioning seemed interesting to some clients, like in the case of Nancy, and if you remember, she wanted more! Sometimes things work out better when we go with the flow, as she suggested. A client's positive feedback made all the difference to this shaky practitioner who was still learning about his abilities. Her helpful input also made me more curious about how healing energy was working on her body. She claimed that she could feel a steady energy flow and was aware visually when it shifted. There were a variety of shapes and colorful energy patterns that appeared and disappeared in front of her. She said they would frequently change in synchronicity with my hand movements. Nancy's observation was way over my head at that time. I was only able to notice some forms and waves, and when the energy flow came to an end, so did the session. My hands dropped down like a puppets. The effectiveness of the treatment was encouraging. We compared her symptoms and general feeling of wellness from before to after. She noticed the discomforts that were present in the beginning had gone and were replaced by a state of joy, peace, and contentment. It was a very encouraging first-time experience in intuitive healing!

"I'm so grateful for the time we had together..."

All credit for the success of this experiment goes to Nancy, my brave client, and to Divine Beings for their supervision and assistance. From that point on, my focus was more on intuition and following the flow of energy. When learning, there is the need to follow a training model or structure, but I found I had the need to rely on faith, or I wouldn't be able to really stretch the boundaries of this gift God had bestowed upon me. It wasn't easy as my faith was frequently tested. There was so much that I wanted to know about this new flow of energy, but since it was something that was finding me, there wasn't anyone to talk to about it. Although there were many people I questioned, the response I received was not enlightening or helpful. Some even seemed intimated by me. When the support from my Reiki group ended, I felt needy, meaning in need of answers, because peculiar things were happening, and these events would be hard for anyone to handle. Imagine someone going to their Reiki master every other day with statements like, "My hands are tapping on my clients because of some strange, ethereal energy. What do I do?" I was in full gear and deeply entrenched in my New Age odyssey at that point. I suppose every trial and error I was experiencing was allowing for self discovery. There were some triumphs in the process too. Certain well-timed, good-times that helped to fuel the journey further. As patterns became more familiar and distinguishable, I began to trust my intuition more. Without any other teaching or external feedback, other than the testimony from clients, I continued on. The more I trusted in the process of intuition, the more intuition came in. And that, my friends, is how it works!

The Maestro

From the outside looking in my skills as an intuitive healer must have seemed comical. I previously stated that my hands and arms made me seem like a conductor orchestrating a symphony, except, instead of the maestro being in control of the music, the music was in control of the maestro. Once the music (energy flow) started, there was no stopping it, not that I wanted to stop it. On most occasions the melody felt wonderful moving through me and too good to stop.

Thankfully, too because each session was forty-five minutes long. Out of curiosity, I tried a few times to stop my hands from moving, but I couldn't. My arms were on auto pilot. After about three months of practice though, the energy flow changed from two arms to one and mostly through the wrist and fingers. I don't believe it was the energy that changed, but more the way I was able to handle it. There was more ease to my movements and obviously more confidence. I felt good about my advancement, and my friends and clients felt great while receiving it.

The energy work must have been beneficial or people wouldn't have been interested in continuing sessions. As success became obvious, I started to feel limitless. I wanted to be open to anyone with every issue they had to bring. While giving a session, the movement of my hands determined whether it was working or not. I wanted to improve when things didn't seem to work as well. I wanted to accommodate everyone who came to me. Sometimes it was enough to just 'get out of the way' of their healing. Wayne Dyer used to say that the word "ego" was an acronym for "Edging God Out!" Improvement always comes when we step out of our human self. If we create obstacles through our fear and doubt then we diminish our ability to stay strong and keep the faith. We need to sometimes get out of our own way and allow grace to flow through us. When we align with one another for the higher good there is always an opportunity for this grace to enter. This is the precise moment that everything falls into place. It's the simple ways God gives us to interact that often go unnoticed. Life becomes too complicated and loud, but eventually when we do finally get out of our way of healing (and do it God's way), everything becomes easier. As with my Reiki practice, allowance was what thrusted me into a higher level of ability. I no longer left anything to my human self to do. I gave all the credit to the powers that were controlling my hands. I was just the vehicle for the energy to flow through. In the end, I realized God was the Maestro, and I was putty in those hands.

Practice Makes Perfect 'Sense'

With much practice came an expansion of energy, but it also caused my senses to expand as well. Energy patterns took shape in my mind's eye, and I could recognize an aura as opened or closed. I would proceed to help it heal, and then close it before the end of a session. I could also see the different etheric bodies, which displayed as layers of color that would emit from a client's aura. This is much like the glow of light (halo) we see surrounding the heads of saints in religious depictions. It is a way of expressing the ethereal body. For example, an enlightened human would most likely have a lot of gold color around their aura, demonstrating the flow of God in them.

I could also tell what part of the body the energy was flowing to. I always stayed in one spot in the middle of the table and facing the client regardless of where the energy was being projected to. When beginning to work on someone, they would list their complaints. "My neck hurts, also my back, and my knee..." I would respond to them by saying, "I don't direct the healing, but let's wait and see." I let them know that I appreciated the direction and trusted that their aches and pains would resolve themselves by the end of the session. Very often there was improvement, which let me know my ability to help in the process was improving as well.

Besides having the occasional distraction of channeling (entities trying to speak to me), advancement was evident. I was also confident that I would eventually break through my own blocks as I continued to search for more answers. I am sure now that my gift of healing would not have come through if I wasn't evolving. The gift spurred more growth, and the growth spurred more gift. It is an ongoing process. Once gift becomes activated, the rest has to do with clearing whatever prevents more activation. 'We' put the limits on it by the way. Be it through fear, conditioning of the mind, ego, control issues, and all other baggage, we hold ourselves back from experiencing advancement. So I was eager to keep driving on this journey! I was excited to see how much more refinement could be accomplished. No matter what I had to grow from or out of, the process made me too excited to stop. Most likely, when we experience something out of the ordinary, we either isolate ourselves and don't look for a logical explanation, or we are desperate to pursue one.

The Pursuit

My only concern was in keeping the intuition flowing and that it remained persistently vibrant. I took notice that each session had a sequence. The flow would first get directed to the aura and the subtle bodies, then an organ or other body parts. It is important to note that there was additional consent given at the very start of every session, although it wasn't oral, and I was never sure exactly how it was going to be expressed. This constant discovery of intuitive behavior and new ways of applying energy was keeping me on my toes, for sure! There was a domino effect going on that was ushering new opportunities to learn. Once, after holding a photograph, I realized I could feel and read the energy of the person in it. Soon after that discovery, I realized I was able to read energy over the phone and while watching TV. Some time after that, I started testing it out it while chatting on the internet.

In pursuit of like-minded people, I would visit New Age chat rooms on the web. Initially lacking confidence to join in, I listened to everyone else's ideas and abilities. The pace was also a little too fast for me to follow. Being a little slow at typing and a lousy speller, it was hard to keep up. By the time I could figure out what to say and then type it, they were already on a different topic. So I would press the backspace button and just type, "Cool," and be done with it. In time I was able to offer quicker responses, and when I felt it was appropriate, I offered healing services. I had a decent response and actually became brave enough to expand my offerings. This new type of internet exchange fueled my ego and need to gain more recognition as well as more knowledge.

Ringing True

On one occasion while visiting a chat room, I noticed that everyone was talking to one person in particular, and it seemed to have been going on for a while. It was all centered on an older man who had constant ringing in his ears for twenty years. As one can imagine, this constant ringing was interfering with his overall well-being, and his entire life was being affected. It was just horrible what this guy was going through for so long. There were a lot of people in the room, but only two were chatting. Both had much sympathy and concern. They were asking logical questions like, "Have you seen a doctor about it?" and he responded, "Yes, I've gone through all the testing one can possibly imagine throughout the years, but nothing they have done or given me to take has taken away the ringing." Then someone asked about Reiki. "Yes, I have, but it didn't do anything for me. I recently went to see someone who did some type of energy work, and he said that he could help me with it, but after a few treatments, still nothing. He even said I had some type of worms in my ears, which I thought was crazy!"

Although fearful, I was always willing to put my work up to the challenge. It took me a little while, but feeling sorry for him, I finally reached out through private message. I did it privately because I didn't want to come off as arrogant or to act disrespectful to the other practitioners. While I waited for his response, I thought about others who refused my help. 'He wouldn't be the first,' I said to myself. I was hesitant because of his doubt and attitude about the potential for healing his condition, not really about the severity of it. If he was convinced that energy healing would not work, it wouldn't work. I wanted a chance to challenge his way of thinking, and that is how I worded the message. I simply stated I was "an intuitive energy worker willing to give it a shot" if he was. Some time later, his response appeared on the screen for all to view. "Thank you, Kiros, for offering, but I don't think anything can help my condition." I wrote back, "OK, but It would only take a couple of minutes, and you have nothing to lose."

That got everyone's attention, and they started to encourage him. "Just do it," "Yeah, nothing to lose," "Do it, man!" Then they were asking me, "Kiros, what are you going to do for him?" I wrote, "Some intuitive energy work." Their responses were all prompting the poor man. It became one of the strangest and most fun I have ever had in the chat rooms. "OK, Kiros," the old man typed, "what do you want me to do?" I took a deep breath (Oh boy, here we go! Be careful what you ask for.) "In a couple of minutes and when I tell you, stop writing, sit comfortably, and close your eyes. Keep them closed for a few minutes. Can you do that?" "Yes, I can," he wrote. "I'll let you know when," I typed and suddenly noticed that everyone else had stopped.

At that point, there were over fifteen maybe twenty visitors all waiting, praying, watching, and anticipating what would happen next. I can't remember his screen name, but I will refer to him now as "Brave Soul." "OK, Brave Soul," I wrote in big letters, "NOW!"

Either it was my own nervousness that I was feeling or tension in the chat room, but it was visually evident by the lack of action on the screen that there was anticipation in the air. I didn't do much but concentrate and send positive, healing intention. As usual, I believed either the energy would come or not. I wasn't trying to direct it either, but I was focusing on Brave Soul's ears. When the energy stopped, I stopped the session, but it took me a little time before I could write anything. I wrote some directions about sleep and rest that I was receiving and hoped that he would open his eyes eventually to see it. As I was about to push the send button, I read, "Ringing in ears is completely gone. Thank you, Kiros! Now I need to log off and go to sleep and get some rest. Thank you, everyone!" And off Brave Soul went. Meanwhile, everyone went nuts typing all sorts of cheer on the screen. That led to more interactions, and before long I had 50 followers and was able to offer healing services for many more people.

There were a couple of disturbing negative and mean interactions with people who, not only refused any form of healing for themselves (not that I tried to force anything on anyone), but were also discouraging others the ability to heal. After some harassment by a naysayer nurse who didn't even believe in God, I decided to end my chatroom visits. I did understand her negativity though. She worked in a hospital surrounded by so much sickness and suffering. She couldn't imagine how God could be present if all that existed. Focusing only at the present state of being, though, and not investigating how these people got there in the first place, does not paint an accurate picture of God and human suffering. If her work involved working with healthy kids in a happy environment, like in a nursery school, perhaps her attitude about life and God might have been different.

It is easy to blame God for all the harsh things that we deal with in our lives, especially if we are not willing to take responsibility for creating any of it ourselves. Truth is usually replaced with opinion when one engages in discussion about religion, God, and politics, so I usually avoid them. It wasn't the first time that I interacted with someone who hated God, but she was relentless, and her words were poisonous. And being harassed for how we feel about God is ridiculous. Who has the time or energy for such nonsense?

Feeling You/Feeling Me

After leaving the internet behind, I found much better, happier ways to stimulate my mind and interests. I wasn't working full-time as a healer, but I still wanted to explore and remain open to the gift. Looking back I could see that my intuitive perception was working synergistically with my empathic awareness. I would often feel people's physical pains, emotional hurts, and other sensations, but I couldn't fully comprehend all of it. It was frustrating then, and it still can be, even now with more awareness. One aspect has gotten better though, I can now distinguish between my emotions and someone else's. To this day, I still have to remind myself to stay shut down when not in assisting mode. In the very beginning for any empath the most difficult aspect is separating emotion...ours from theirs. Sometimes it is obvious. To give an example, when we are young, we feel healthy and our heart is strong, so it would be easy to recognize if we were about to have a heart attack and standing next to an elderly person, chances are it is not our heart that has an issue.

Besides separating emotions and physical sensations, it is hard to separate information. An empath can be in a room full of people and start receiving insight but won't know who the information is for. There is not much they can do about it either; it just happens. The best anyone can do is to make note of it as it happens, and say a prayer. As it is being noted, by the way, it is stimulating the growth process. In the beginning of understanding, there usually isn't enough trust in our ability to step fully into the role while we are out and about involved in life. It is easier, though, to distinguish energy bodies during a healing session. When a facilitator is in healing mode and in the energy space, everything is more clear. That doesn't mean that every bit of information coming in should be shared. An intuitive will actually sense if it is appropriate to tell someone what they themselves are hearing. It could be that information is coming in for just the practitioner to hear in order to help facilitate the healing process.

There are times when the messages can get out of control too. Imagine being at the supermarket, mall, a restaurant, on a train, at a family gathering, at work, talking on the phone, even walking down the street and feeling things, hearing messages or voices. It can also be annoying to others to constantly be in the space. Sometimes, people don't want to talk about their problems, answer questions or be reminded that they do have an issue. Imagine being asked, "Does your back hurt? What's going on with you? You feel sad? Is your heart OK?" Discussion of whether they feel this or that based on what I am feeling may not prove fruitful! It is especially not recommended to tell a stranger what is being felt. There is a chance of being thought of as crazy. Eventually, everything gets balanced out as each empath and the people (s)he is trying to help find their way.

Stan the Man With the Heart Problems

I was working at my regular job and feeling all kinds of heart problems stemming from "Stan," a client I was in close contact with. I knew from previous experience that this feeling wasn't good. It was loud, which meant something was brewing. Every time I would get in contact with him, either in person or over the phone, I would feel the same sensations. It is really interesting to know how unaware the person is of anything that is going on with me as an empath, even though I am sensing all this stuff going on with them. The person could be ready to have a heart attack, and I have the pain, but they feel nothing. In this case, I sense that I would lose Stan as a client if I said anything, so I thought to talk about general health instead. I started hinting about how important it is to get a regular checkup. Then, I went on to make up an elaborate story about my uncle that didn't listen to his body's signals and symptoms and wound up having a massive heart attack. I kept this exchange going, but in the end, he said his health was fine and he felt great. Frustrated, I said a prayer for him and let it go.

A couple months later, his wife calls to tell us that he was recovering from a triple bypass. Thank God, he was doing okay! It was at these frequent and uncomfortable moments that I questioned my responsibilities as a healer. Not long after that, I was in a meeting with a potential client, and my manager and I realized I was having difficulty focusing. All of a sudden I got the feeling someone's life was coming to an end. It wasn't that often that I would get this feeling, and who wants to accept it no matter how loud the message might be. I was in a meeting full of vibrant people, laughing, talking, exchanging thoughts and ideas, and making business plans. The last thing I wanted to connect with was death. Later on that day, my manager questioned my efforts at the meeting. I told him what I felt, but he didn't accept my explanation. A week later we were informed of the sudden death of that same person. My boss and I were both shocked about his death, but even more so by my ability to sense his demise.

Relying on Full-Time Intuition

I left that job not long after that incident. It wasn't easy to drop that income, and it was probably not the smartest thing to do, but I followed my heart. I had been practicing healing on a part-time basis for about six years and mostly pro bono. Financially speaking, it didn't make sense to try to make a full-time living doing the healing work. Not that there wasn't money to be made, but I didn't have the confidence, and I was afraid of the responsibility that being a healer insinuated. Of course one doubt made the other worse. The stigma attached didn't help either. When I told friends and family that I was an intuitive healer, I would hear, "Get out. You serious?" Then others would join in the conversation, "Yeah, he's a healer," followed by lots of laughing, then "Can you tell something about me with your mind?" After responding, "Do you really want to know?" I told one of them, "Okay, I'm getting a lot of tightness around your heart, and if I were you, I would go and get that checked. Also, you are eating too much junk food that is really bad for you. Consider changing your diet!" More laughter, and the response, "What are you talking about? I'm in perfect health. I have no tightness in my heart! Are you kidding me? I play soccer twice a week, no way." "Well, you asked me," I murmured back, "and that's what I got."

Three months later, I heard he had a massive heart attack while playing soccer and had to be resuscitated with shock paddles. Once in a while I run into him, and he hasn't been able to look at me the same way since, nor has he spoken to me about any of it. Maybe he is afraid of what I might see or say. Ignorance is not a virtue, and people should want to know, but then again, if the shoe was on the other foot I wonder if I would want to know. I am pretty sure I would. Still, it is very frustrating to know how to help and not be allowed to. It makes me wonder, if there was a better way, perhaps a less obtrusive and invasive way. Can people be more open and receptive to healing if I filtered the message better? Of all the ways I've tried throughout the years to soften the blow, nothing has ever worked well enough for me to actually say, "Ahhhhh! That's the missing link!"

Validation is Sometimes Painful

Similar scenarios were happening with potential clients too. My work was recommended to someone who had serious intestinal problems. "Judy" just came over from Europe the day before, and the flight irritated her existing condition. I don't remember the condition specifically, but it wasn't something very common like an ulcer. It didn't matter, though, because I'd never offer specific treatment or diagnosis. I consider that the job of a doctor or health professional. I only offer the energy that the body can (if it chooses to) use to rejuvenate and heal itself. In this case, that energy download happened quickly. Only about ten minutes from start to finish. During the entire session, Judy was squirming on the table from the intense pain, but afterwards she felt no pain or discomfort. I considered it a success. She said thank you and goodnight, nothing else. I thought perhaps she was exhausted from all the pain she had experienced.

A month later I happened to run into both her and her fiancé at the supermarket. I said hello and my greeting was ignored. At first I assumed she didn't recognize me, but her energetic vibes let me know she did. I had no idea what was going on in her mind, but I assumed the session didn't help her that much. Finally, her fiancé saw me and offered a hello, so I walked towards them and asked her how she was feeling. She completely ignored me and my question. Feeling slighted and confused, I made a polite notion to her fiancé, "She doesn't remember me?" "No, I remember you!" she yelled back in anger. "What did you do to me? You waved your hand over me for a few minutes, and what I've been suffering with for four years now is all gone? Why? . . . And the doctors have been poking me and poking me, and everything they have done to me for years . . . and all the tests? Nothing ever helped me."

Taken by complete surprise, I stood there and replied, "I don't know what I did or what your doctors have been doing to you. All I can say is that you should be grateful that you have your health." She looked at me, then fuming, put her head down like a bull and charged out the exit. Her fiancé followed her out, shaking his head and yelling, "That's what I've been telling her all along." Now I'm shaking my head thinking she needed an exorcism. Perhaps she was using suffering as a tool, a weapon or an excuse...I'm not sure. This kind of behavior makes me wonder what comes first, the misery or the problem? But after thinking about it, I realized there might not have been a true healing of the underlying causes. The energy work may have only cleared the surface issue of body pain. If Judy's healing was done properly, she would have been able to hold her new space. The patterns of imbalance exposed through that healing session showed her challenges were too much for her to bear without the physical pain. Pain made more 'sense' to her. Back in the day, I would have said, "I don't get it?" but I understand so much more about the conscious and subconscious minds now.

From the healer's perspective, a quick fix is very gratifying for the ego, but it may not be what the doctor ordered for some patients. Knowing we helped someone heal may actually perpetuate and instigate more of an ego battle. If this challenge is about self worth and self esteem, it will generate questions, like, "Am I really a healer?" and "Why me?" Nothing seems to satisfy lack of self worth and esteem, because we as humans find it so difficult to believe in our own unique specialness. If healing capabilities were taken away, would the healer still feel special? It is important to remember that we are all special, regardless of our ability to facilitate healing.

Strength in Numbers or Just Overbearing?

Some years back I was invited to work on about ten people at once. One-on-one sessions are private and confidential. Healing done in groups is entirely more complicated. When there is an audience and no confidentiality, there is inhibition and there is also a lot of expectation and pressure placed on the healer to perform. To my surprise, when I got to the group session, the room was filled with people I knew but hadn't seen in many years. It was equally surprising to them to see me since no one told them who the healer was. In the corner of the room sat a man named Tom, one of the few people I didn't know. Tom had recently suffered a stroke and was there for a desperately needed healing. The stroke caused immobility and pain in his arm, which was strapped to his body, and his leg dragged when he walked. I was very familiar with strokes and the pain they caused, because my father had one when I was seventeen. Since Tom was in so much pain, I worked on him first. He hobbled over to the table, so I took care to help him get comfortable. Then I took my usual place at the middle of the table and placed my hands in position. Thankfully, the energy started flowing right away without me needing to direct it. I was tenuous about being in this room with all of these people, but I knew it wasn't about them. My faith was being tested, along with my ability to let go of my ego.

Feelings of unworthiness, lack of confidence and self esteem can make us seek exterior validation over and over again. No matter how many apparent breakthroughs we undergo, we seem to always need more validation that we are doing okay. I have been in this space before, as well as being on the spot, but this time it was in front of friends.

Everyone knows news travels quickly, and I didn't want it to be bad news. I had been standing over Tom for a short while when my hand stopped moving. I moved it voluntarily, knowing full well no one could tell the difference. I used the time to think of answers I might be asked. Feeling anxious, I wanted the whole thing over, but I didn't want to undermine Tom's healing. When the session ended I told him to take his time getting up. As he stood I asked, "How do you feel?" I know it is impossible, but I could swear I felt everyone's breath on the back of my neck. At that moment, Tom begins to share his before and after results. "I have no more pain in my arm, and the burning sensation is gone. It is the same with my leg." Of course I had immediate relief hearing this! These were great results for a first time treatment. More relaxed at that point, I guided him toward a chair and told him to rest for a while. I ended with, "I'll check if more energy comes in for you a little later."

Before his butt reached the seat, everyone charged at him, asking questions about what he felt. I just continued on with the next person, oblivious to what was going on. At some point Tom left saying he would come back for his follow up. While I was working on the fourth person, he came back toward the house, but passed by without entering. Some people caught sight of him almost running down the block with his cane over his shoulder, much like a soldier holds his gun while marching. It was a peculiar but exciting moment. No one understood why he was running, but it was obvious there was a transformation. We all laughed, "Why isn't he coming in?" We would know the answer soon enough.

When people are desperate, they say desperate things. Before I began work on Tom, he promised to give me his pension check if I could heal him. He had no clue, but I was so relieved to perform well in front of all those friends that I would have paid him if he got up and walked out without the cane! Poor Tom, he couldn't even say thank you, let alone come back to face me and pay what he had offered. And he wasn't the only one who would disparage me that day. I was told later that six out the ten on lookers made negative comments about me and my work. I was thankful they all knew Tom and his plight, or they might have thought I planted him there. Looking back, I realize that the energy of the room before I even started was enough to make me anxious. People want to judge. Some want others to fail, and it is not because they care about what others are doing as much as they care that they can't seem to move forward themselves. I expected more enthusiasm from everyone when they witnessed Tom's return to health, and that is my ego issue as well. The event took its toll on me, and the good that came out of no good was part of my personal journey. I needed to remember that awesome feeling of being a facilitator, whether there is a healing or not. And who is to say anyway? A healing is between the recipient and The Divine, irrespective of who is facilitating it.

Healing Power?

Many people I have encountered through the years do not feel fully present in their power. Most likely it is because there is so much more advancement that can be achieved than any one of us can realize. While on the journey of self enlightenment, we are seekers, and sometimes we don't appreciate what we have already found. We just keep seeking and thinking we haven't found "it" yet. All of this can leave us a little empty if we allow it. But it also leaves us without a leader. An old saying in Greece, "A one-eyed person is king to the multitudes that are blind". Very few teachers and healers are actually out there to harm or hold anyone back from their own healing process, but when a weakened healer feels lost in the notion that they are not powerful, there is a tendency to keep giving away more of their energy in hopes of a quick fix. They may give away whatever they have left to a promise maker (an energy worker who may not be in alignment with a higher power) in their zeal to advance, but without seeing the possible repercussions.

Sometimes it is hard not to take two steps back for every one step we move forward.

Although I had some major breakthroughs in this area, I was still looking for more and more validation. My intuition, psychic ability and clairvoyance were advancing, which meant I was also advancing in awareness, but on a personal level, I didn't feel a growth that I could measure. I still questioned my integrity and felt a struggle gaining confidence, empowerment, self love and self worth. When we are in this default state of mind but still decidedly willing to move forward, we will attract what we need to help us. People, places, therapies, information... whatever form it comes in, we will be drawn to it and it will be drawn to us. It might seem that the teachers that are put on our path are in better shape than us, but actually that may not be true. They might be at the same level or state of being, but are supported by others that are helping them. Maintaining forward movement while not becoming lost in the process should be our goal. When any one of us finds ourselves tumbling down instead of climbing up, we need to take a closer look at the people who are helping us on the hike. Meditate on the question: Are they really helping me move on or am I still stuck?

"The Power of Now," by Eckhart Tolle: *"True salvation is to 'know God'—not as something outside you, but as your innermost essence. True salvation is to know yourself as an inseparable part of the timeless and formless One Life from which all that exists derives its being."*

Long-Distance Healing (LDH)

At a certain point in my healing practice my hands-on work was down to 10%. It was due to the long-distance healing work I was doing over the phone. Having been on the recipient end of this type of healing and then doing my own work through the internet, I had no problem believing how effective it was. I used LDH on people that had knees that supposedly required surgery, back problems, emotional issues, fears and phobias. All seemed to significantly improve after treatment, but doubt that I was the one facilitating the healing always persisted. Validation, validation, validation...seemed it was always necessary. Irrespective of this, my LDH odyssey continued, and I became really proficient as I learned better ways to deal with distractions. When on a call with a client, I found it easier to keep the focus and attention on them. What I was feeling and picking up ethereally was coming only from them and the people they were concerned about. Very little from my ego or about anything else entered my mind. Funny how the phone 'disconnected' me from my stuff as it 'connected' me to theirs.

Of course my monkey mind wasn't satisfied with this. I wanted to have more fun and make things more complicated. I started to think, 'If I can facilitate LDH over the internet and on the phone, why not over the TV or even sending it to people in need and in every part of the world?' Now, I wasn't imaging myself sitting in a room all day meditating and focusing on healing the world. That wasn't it at all. Through the years, though, I have prayed and meditated alone, trying to help world situations that resonated with me. Truthfully, a healing energy is created when we meditate on the world in a positive state of unconditional love and peace. If we all did this, perhaps everyone would learn quicker and issues would dissolve. I already know this kind of thinking helps us connect to people in our immediate circle. I really want to believe we can influence people we have never met as well.

Can Our Prayers Put a Dent in the Suffering?

I think about the children in sweatshops, the sick laying in hospital beds, the hungry and abused, the mistreated people and animals of the world...I really do. Eventually, I believe we will have no other alternative but to unite as a big family and share our common ground. The spiritual evolution is necessary to pick us up out of the despair. I have much gratitude to all those who have elevated their awareness and realized their need to help the rest of us with their prayers. Many are already hard at work to help others soften their path of self discovery. They recognize the need to light the torch and lead the way, and in the process of this individual growth, everyone will be able to pull each other forward in unity. It is in this unity that we will find ultimate healing for the world.

When I pray and meditate for all of humanity, I concentrate on harmony for us here on Earth and our need to undo the ways we harm this planet and its inhabitants. I pray for all of us to take responsibility for our own past and present endeavors and stop blaming others (most especially, God) for how we got to where we landed. Often while doing these prayer/meditations, new ideas would enter my head; methods we could use to do mass healings through LDH. I once thought that I stumbled onto something big, so I tried to expand upon it. While watching the news one night, an anchor reported on an actor that I loved since childhood and had met once. He was in a coma, on life support for twenty-four hours and not expected to live. It sounded really gloomy, but I got the notion that this actor was not done performing yet. I decided to send him some LDH energy. 'Why not,' I said to myself. 'What have either of us to lose?'

Sitting comfortably on my couch, I tuned into this man by thinking about him and visualizing him in my head. Once I felt the connection, I asked God to please help him if it was meant to be. As I did, I could feel the energy move through me, but I stayed focused and then felt the shift in its flow. Of course, I didn't have this man's consent (which would have made it easier), but asking for God's will made it legitimate, nonetheless. The energy moved through me in the usual manner, and again, like all other sessions I had done, the energy stopped and the session ended. And that's all I did. A day or two later, he completely recovered. Of course I didn't really believe that I had anything to do with it, but I mentioned the coincidence to my close friend, "Rita," just to see her reaction and satisfy my ego.

On or about a year later, the actor was on the news again. He was sick, but apparently not as sick as the previous incident. It wasn't portrayed as dramatic, but still news worthy. I decided to send him some LDH energy once again. This time, though, I was well aware of my ego. I wanted to know! I knew it wasn't healthy to feel this way, but deep down I needed validation. I got into position on the couch, made the connection with him and then God. It was the same as before, but what I experienced following my routine was definitely not routine.

"Sometimes, death is healing."

As I was focusing and welcoming the energy, a vision came to me of an endless, blue sky with many puffy clouds, and on each one was an Angel. I heard a loud but gentle voice in my head as clear as it would be if I heard with my ears, "You can't help him this time. He's with us." All of it took me by surprise, but I couldn't think to say anything but, "Oops!" There were all sorts of mixed thoughts and emotions as I tried to take it all in. I have seen Angels before but never so many at once and too many to even count. Even ones that were at a distance were still visible. It was an amazing vision, and I was blown away completely. I shared the vision with Rita. "All that I can say is that, considering from what I saw and felt, he's going to have a great transitioning." He did pass on, but I don't remember how soon after.

A year later Rita called to tell me she saw the actor's daughter on television speaking about her father's life, his great passion and the long career he had in theatre and movies. She also spoke of how he loved the people he worked with and always supported newcomers and all who needed his help. She said he was known for his good heart and generosity, always first to assist and to provide. "Everyone that knew him loved him," she said, "and he loved everyone. He died in his sleep while traveling to the island of Rhodes to do what he loved best...perform in the theatre." I was thrilled to hear he died like a Viking with fire still in his heart!

The Greek actor wasn't the first well-known or popular person I was guided to help over the years. Recently, while watching reruns, I was reminded of another actor I worked on in a similar way about fifteen years prior. I saw his death as well. Sometimes I felt drawn to help souls (famous or not) almost as if they were asking me, even though we never met in person. Obviously I can't prove any of it, and without their testimony, I only have my side of the story. These LDH experiments were interesting, as healing wasn't the only focus. Sometimes I would offer advice and emotional support. Once I even gave an idea for a movie (more on that later). I can imagine how crazy all of this sounds to you, my readers, but at that time I wanted to push the theory to the max. There is scientific evidence that proves that prayer done by the masses has reduced crime. They did this experiment in Washington, DC and convinced an entire police department how well it can work.

I didn't know how effective I was at LDH. No one was able to attest to it, but one incident made me sit up and take notice. I had been getting persistent messages about Christopher Reeve that were frustrating and a little intimidating. I never had to worry about the energy that LDH created before, but this time it was different. I tried to ignore the messages, and every time the image of him was placed in my head, I would ask for a healing for him. Usually that would be enough to satisfy the promptings, but it got to a point that it wasn't. More requests would come in repeatedly, and they would come with a desperate need to reach out to him. I wasn't sure what source was creating it, but it felt like a crazy obsession, and I wanted to put an end to it. The requests came in as thoughts, voices, dreams, and all were trying to get me to do the same thing: Get to him! I finally searched out his foundation and emailed them.

My name is Kiros, and I'm trying to get in touch with Mr. Reeves. I'm not sure this is the right e-mail address, but if you can give him the message, it would be helpful and appreciated. If you can tell him that I'm a spiritual healer and that someone close to him has strong faith that he can recover, and so do I. There are a lot of whys and hows, but the overwhelming need to offer my assistance is stronger. So I'm offering my assistance with an open heart and strong faith. God bless.

I didn't expect anyone to take it seriously, but I had to put it out there. In doing so, I finally got released, and that felt good. I let the source that prompted the request know that I did it with positive intention. Soon after, I was surprised to get a response thanking me for my concern and offer to assist. They said the message was forwarded to his personal assistant who would get in touch with me if they were interested. I didn't hear anything from his assistant or anyone else. I would never profess to know that I could help him, but I wanted so much to try. A month later, he passed on. Sadly, I blamed myself for not being more professional about it, and for all the other times I was too afraid to reach out to people I was spiritually led to.

Even though I didn't connect with many of the famous people that I received messages for, I still felt the need to follow through on trying to heal them. When messages about Clint Eastwood started coming in, I was excited to help, because he was (and still is) one of my favorite actors. Without his knowledge, I did many sessions for him over a few months span, and one day I was surprised to start receiving the writing for an actual screen play. As this experience was happening, it seemed as crazy to me as I am sure it does to you reading it now, but I went through with it anyway. While praying for him, I started to talk to his soul about the story line that I was seeing and hearing. Eventually the visions and voices stopped, and I completely forgot about the entire event. Some time later, when I saw him being interviewed on a talk show, he commented about a recent health condition that was interfering with his memory and ability to work and write. I perked up after hearing him mention the time frame and realized it was simultaneous with the healing work I did for him. It was not long after that he started to write prolifically and produce many great movies. I would love to think I had a hand in that, but again, coincidence plays it role in my doubt process.

Over the years while living in New York, I had come to meet and shake hands with many famous people like Anthony Quinn, Richard Harris, Jack Nicholson, Liv Tyler, Joaquin Phoenix, Jack Scalia, and Robert De Niro, to name just a few. If I had the egotistical need to assist celebrities in any way, I could have reached out many times, but no impressions or visions of them every came to me. And that is why I believe the messages that do come in are real. Not that long ago, thoughts about someone I had met many years prior were coming in. I didn't know how to reach out to them, but am actually happy that I didn't. What do I say to someone when I know they are going to die, "Hello, remember me? I got a message you are passing on soon, so go take care of business." I would have also told them that I tried to help, but I couldn't, although who knows if doing this energy work isn't helping their transition? The passing of this person did take place, by the way, two months after my vision.

Barbara's Blight

A couple of years after the healing with Tom, "The running man," I got some visions about two of the other people who were also part of the circle, namely; siblings Nancy and Rob. The undertones of these visions though were not good, and I didn't want to get in touch with either of them. Out of obligation to their souls and because of the seriousness of the messages I was receiving, I told their sister, Barbara, who hosted the event. Without sounding grave, I told her what I was hearing and asked that she pass on the message. I also offered to assist in their healing process if they chose to heed the message. Barbara didn't tell me their exact words, but I know they all considered my offer to be silly. The visions came back a month later, and again I felt compelled to do something, so I swallowed my pride and risked humiliation. Better that though than guilt, and besides, there was more to be concerned about, so I was much more specific this time with her about the messages.

Barbara got upset with the information I gave her about Nancy, but knowing that her sister would not have taken it seriously, she reiterated to me what Nancy had to say about my last vision. I tried to persuade Barbara to talk her sister into at least getting checked out. I have never been on the receiving end of this kind of information, but I would think if someone told me that I may have a serious health concern that feels energetically like cancer, I would be booking my doctor appointments to at least rule it out. Barbara could not convince her sister. Within a year, both her brother and sister passed away, and that was after her older sister the year before. It was a horrible time for her.

Shortly after, she called distressed and in need of my help. "Please come, there is something not right with me! I ate something, and my intestine has been killing me for days." I reminded her that I wasn't a medical professional and it sounded to me like she needed to get to a hospital. "Let me talk to your son or whoever is with you now," I told her. Apparently, her family was trying to take her to the emergency room for two days, but she was too afraid to go. She feared the worst and who could blame her? She wanted to escape that fear by having me come to lay hands on her to see if anything was seriously wrong. I decided to appease her by going, but also to persuade her to get to the hospital. I didn't tell her that I had a vision about her just a month before.

Needless to say, by the time I arrived, she didn't look well at all, and her energy felt weak. I didn't want to do anything that would make her feel too comfortable knowing it would give her an excuse to stay home.

Because of the vision I had about her health, I was unsure how to proceed. I decided to just stay centered and neutral from everyone's fear, but still open and ready to facilitate if that was what I was being led to do. Barbara had a desperate need to keep asking me if she was going to be okay and if I saw anything of concern. Finally at my urging she went to the hospital, but only after I promised I would come to see her the next day.

At the hospital the staff ran all the necessary tests. The results that came in were not good. There was a growth the size of a small orange in the abdominal area. Her fears were materializing, and she was in a state of panic by the time I arrived at the hospital the next day. Even though it was not confirmed as cancer, the doctor and her family wanted her to get a test only Sloan Kettering (the cancer hospital in New York City) offered. During all of this, she and her family were looking to me for answers and comfort. Since I was dead on about her siblings, it made sense that I might be able to tune in to her condition and its severity. I remained reserved and kept everything basic, but decided to do some hands on work to facilitate her healing. After starting the Reiki, I began to receive visions of the large mass in her abdomen breaking apart, but I didn't want to say anything about what I was seeing. It was not my place to aid in the prognosis, but I still wanted to offer comfort. The only bit of information that really resonated with me was that she needed IV fluids and that would help with discharging the mass. Her questions were persistent. "What do you think Kiros? Am I going to make it? It is bad, isn't it? You don't want to tell me, do you!" She kept crying and I kept reassuring her. "Not at all!" I told her. "The best thing you did was come to the hospital and get hydrated. Now it is a matter of time for your body to get rid of this thing. Just wait and see." She had faith in my statements and started to become optimistic, offering support to her family. "What are you getting upset about? You heard what he said, I'm going to get rid of it!" I finally left when I saw her spirits rising.

The next night I got a call from a screaming woman and at first couldn't make out who it was. When I realized it was Barbara screaming with joy, I perked up. Turns out that the testing done at Sloan Kettering the next day proved that the mass had indeed dissolved overnight, and there was no sign of its existence. All that was needed was the insertion of a tube to drain the liquid that remained. Every time I ran into her after the episode, she would thank me for, as she put it, "Saving her life." "If it wasn't for you, Kiros, they would have gotten me." I would remind her that I don't do the saving. "I'm just the messenger delivering what is there for you already." It's been awhile since I have seen her, but I have it on good authority that she is doing well.

"There are two ways to live your life. One is as though nothing is a miracle. The other is as though everything is a miracle."

—ALBERT EINSTEIN

"When it is time to go…!"

When our bodies heal and find a way to recover, whether it was from a treatment, a practitioner or any other reason, it is because it was not our time to leave here. I have written many times that a treatment that works for one may not work for another. At this point in the book, I am hoping I made my point clear about why some heal and some don't. There are so many variables to uncover in the sickness and healing process with too many reasons why someone would remain ill. Marketing healing mechanisms like Reiki is important since a lot of people are not aware of what they are or that they can be effective. I'm not sure of the national statistics of people who use complimentary and alternative treatments versus customary, but I'm guessing the percentages are much higher than fifty years ago. Even so, it would be difficult to extrapolate a cure rate for alternative medicine.

Traditional medicine concerns itself with symptoms, not cures and causes. Western and traditional medicine believe that if you are walking and breathing, you are still alive. If you can eat and watch TV, then the meds worked. None of the medical techniques that are used on the body dabble in self-awareness, empowerment, spiritual potential, and inner knowing. The medical society is convinced that the mental and emotional state of the mind and heart are influencing the body, but they are not doing anything to direct their attention to either! They are still trying to sell pills to fix what is going on in the energy body. The misalignment of the body with the mind and the spirit is where all the discomfort and disease reside, and until we start uncovering these causes, most of what we do will be unsuccessful or if successful, only temporary.

Missing Pieces

Discovering the mysteries of life (and in particular, my life's purpose) has been my personal quest, and both have inspired an endless variety of questions, ideas and thoughts over the years. I have learned consistently, and so these ideas and concepts change as my perception changes. Not to say that I am crystal clear on everything yet, but I have so much knowingness about certain things that have been downloaded through the years, and I have a great desire to share them. I like to think of life as a puzzle undone, and like any puzzle, the picture only becomes clear when many pieces have been put together. As life unfolds, so too does our picture on the puzzle. Every experience of personal growth acts like a piece that we can put into its space allowing us to see who we truly are. When each life cycle begins, the collection of the pieces that make us are strewn around, waiting for us to put them into place. There are pieces with names like, "growing up," "doing the right thing," "living our life," "making plans," "writing goals," "being part of life," "having a life," "making a family," "having a career," "being happy," "being creative in life…" All of what we consider wonderful reasons to engage and strive for fulfillment here on Earth. A small list for sure, but feel free to add whatever you like!

If we succeed in any or all of them, we become more at peace with ourselves. On the other hand, if we fail, we default on the self image. Considering we are told from a very young age what we should have and do in order to be happy, we automatically believe we fail when we don't 'have it all.' We even mimic what we consider 'happy people' and use them as role models, trying to live the same way, buy the same cars, houses, clothes, etc. All this is done for the sake of happiness. Meanwhile our own puzzle is undone. When a piece of our puzzle does fit into our picture, we sometimes disregard its importance. If we have to struggle with the puzzle, we leave it alone for a while. Some things draw our attention away. Imagine how a new BMW holds our attention far more easily than a silly puzzle piece. Looking back at my puzzle, there were no hot cars, but there were plenty of people that held my attention! There were also plenty of situations that made me look the other way at the pieces that were trying to find their way to come together. These distractions all played their role in creating the delays in my personal growth. My puzzle has lots of finished areas now, and it is showing me a magnificent flow of life. There are many tears of joy and sadness expressed in it, but it is all good.

A Human Life Starts with a Breath

Being slapped in the rear end is an abrupt way to be awakened to live and breath, and perhaps it is the first indication of what cruelty awaits us! I am sure it leaves a lasting impression. Hmmm, perhaps that is why most of us still need a kick in the rear on occasion...? Nonetheless, our entry point is painful, which says a lot about what life here will be. No matter the whys and hows of the birth process, behind it all still exists the fact that we brought ourselves here! And once we arrive, from that first breath, our life becomes a cycle in motion. There is a reason why every situation occurs. Our life, albeit easy or rough, inspires growth through all its nuances; using the people around us, and all situations we find ourselves in to move us in various directions. All of them play their part in our expansion from a physical, emotional, mental, and spiritual perspective, inspiring our every reaction, thought, and emotion. This all happens with or without our knowledge (although it is likely our soul's gave prior consent) as we interact with each other and live through the subsequent drama. These life lessons are unique and played out through our individual expression.

As me move forward and discover the tools that have been granted us since birth, we become more proficient at uncovering ourselves and who we are. This unveiling may be slow, as who we are and what we can become may not be apparent early on. Life, parents and situations can mold us into a shape that may be less than who we were meant to be. That is okay though, because life is meant to be a constant learning platform. We get to take as long as we want, and it most definitely will take as long as we allow. It is up to us how fast or slow we move through the process. As we do this, the picture of that puzzle exists without physical form, potentially dormant and waiting for the opportunity to be fully revealed. In time, one way or another, our buttons get pushed and our triggers gradually activate. It is up to us to find those triggers and to recognize that they are not the same as everyone else's. We need to figure out where they originate so we can rid ourselves of them.

"From the first breath of life, life is set in motion...your life, and there is no turning back. The clock is ticking. Life is moving speedily forward in the physical and hopefully equally so in the spiritual. No time to look back now. Right? Not so! In order to move forward, we will sometimes have to look back."

—Kiros

My Final Thoughts...

Let's face it; none of us are perfect, but we are perfectly made! We have all been on both sides, but we don't have to take sides. We have been given tools, but it takes a lifetime to learn how to use them. It is all about the growth! It is all about the bigger picture of who we truly are. Living, experiencing, and creating...this is the master plan. Not many aspects of life fall into place at the time we have it marked on our calendar, but as I look back on my life, I realize that it was my plan. Just as air provides for each breath, so is life providing us with the tools.

Breathe, my friends!

Testimonials

I saw colors, patterns, and forms as Kiros worked over me—something I didn't expect to happen. First, as he began to work, I saw intricate moving patterns of bluish-gray light, which became stronger and less gray as he went on. They were both geometric and organic patterns. After he stopped and then resumed his hand movements, I noticed a light flash out from his hand—almost a neon color bluish, greenish purple. Then the patterns changed to softer forms—cloud-like— misty and became more pinkish or purple. Beneath the patterns existed a golden field of light that shifted in and out. Afterward, I felt very relaxed, and my voice (with a paralyzed vocal cord) was remarkably stronger.

Jacqui T. B.

I first saw Kiros at a psychic seminar shaking his hands over the body of a person who was relaxing upon a massage table. I took the opportunity to meet with him, both out of curiosity and a need to relax for a while in the middle of an interesting, but very busy and exhausting day. While I felt some unusual energy during my time with Kiros, I felt no different either in body or mind. It was not until a full twenty-four hours later that I realized I had been literally walking around for hours completely free of the knee and hip joint pain, which had been a constant reminder of the fact that I do have arthritis. I was regularly visiting an orthopedist for my arthritic problems, and I had used my prescription for Vioxx for quite some time, but none of this has helped me as much as my visit with Kiros.

Nancy L.

A few hours after my treatment with Kiros, the pain was gone. I was able to walk without my cane, and I was able to go up and down the stairs on my own. The next day I was back to work and have been working ever since. Thank's to Kiros' encouraging words and healing hands!

P.S. Queens, NY

Back in September of 2009, I was suffering with severe medical problems. My mom recommended that I speak with Kiros. It has been a year since, and having the privilege to work with such a gifted individual has led me to understand how my emotions, in part, contributed to my ill health. What I thought was the reality of my life, Kiros had the ability to cut through to the true and deep underlying issues. Through non-judgment, patience, a bit of humor, and a very generous spirit, he has led me to uncover the authentic individual that I was created to be. He has helped me to enhance my own intuition so that I can see, hear and feel myself much more clearly, thus enabling my ability to create a healthier life.

R.H., C.O

I had a loud ringing in my ears for more than a month. Because of the loud ringing I couldn't sleep, relax and I was very nervous. Certain sounds were very irritating and I also was under constant unknown fears. After a few sessions with Kiros, I was able to sleep, relax, and all the fears seemed to be gone. At the same time the loud ringing was gradually disappeared. Most importantly, I became more balanced and peaceful! Words cannot express my gratitude and the way I feel now after these sessions with Kiros."A.D. Queens, NY

I met Kiros right after being diagnosed with lymphoma for the third time. I began treatments with him without really knowing what to expect, but having an intuitive feeling that he would be able to help me through. He is a very special healer, as I have experienced major transformations both spiritually and emotionally. There were various times that my body was so swollen from the drug therapy that I was unable to be touched by either a massage therapist, acupuncturist or amma therapist. That is when I depended upon Kiros for his healing techniques. Each session was different and more effective than the next. I could immediately feel the swelling and pain diminish, as well as a deep relaxation and calming effect. I am grateful that I met him! He is a warm, compassionate healer who has been invaluable to me."

J.E. Massage Therapist, Special Education Teacher - Seaford, NY

Kiros has done wonderful healing work on myself and my son, Frank. When I met him, I had problems with my knee, but since having his treatments, my knee has improved, and I have no pain. Even better, my son was diagnosed with visual perceptual problems, which caused him great learning difficulty. Since Kiros started working on him, his vision became normal and his grades improved from a D to a B average. I cannot express in words how much we appreciate his work!

Veronica S. Queens, NY

I am a massage therapist and after injuring my elbow, I needed treatment fast. The pain was so severe that it was affecting my work. After my first session with Kiros, the pain was gone, and I mean gone! The next day it came back, but not as severe. It took three more visits, but the pain completely vanished. His treatment really works!

K.G. Massage Therapist, Queens, NY

Notes

Notes